SELECTING A NETWORK MARKETING OPPORTUNITY:
AN INSIDER'S APPROACH

By:
Ryan Daley

Alpine, Utah, USA

ISBN 1450561160
LCCN 978145056117

Printed in the United States of America.

PREFACE

This book has been in the process of being written for a number of years. Many of the sections contained within this book are mini-trainings that I have taught throughout my consulting experiences to distributors, neighbors, industry leaders, corporate management teams, and frankly anyone who had a question about the industry as a whole.

I love network marketing, and I hope that this fact is seen in this text. I also am not blind to aspects in network marketing that other people don't like; and their concerns are often valid. The bulk of this book was developed during a time when I was tired of what half the industry was doing to their distributors – and I found myself teaching more and more people what to look for, what the right questions were to ask, and how to help them find the right company for themselves. Eventually I found myself an opportunity that I loved, and I could no longer consult as regularly as I felt it was necessary to help the industry evolve as a whole – and I felt that fact hastened the need for this text.

I also love the world of research, behavior, and academics. I hope that all my books that are published will help to legitimize the field of research in network marketing and behavior, as well as help refine the actions and tactics that are used in the industry. Companies will do what works and creates revenue – but revenue is determined by what their distributors do and accept. I hope that all of my texts, including this book (being my first), will also help every reader make an unbiased and educated decision in the choices they make in selecting the network marketing company for them.

If each distributor can make more informed decisions, that single action will refine the industry, change the behavior of the industry, and help the industry as a whole reach the potential and power that is inherent in its nature. Network marketing can change the world, should change the world, and one day really will change the world (more so than it already has).

As stated above, much of this was written over a number of years, but with that said, I feel it is important to emphasize that much of this book has been written with the attempt of giving an unbiased perspective. Therefore, you will notice that throughout this book I do not advocate one principle above another, but only offer considerations in regard to that principle when it is being reviewed by the potential distributor.

Everyone is different, and throughout this text the reader will find that the level of honestly about the industry presented will show more respect to the difference of each individual than for the industry itself. People are people, and people are important. People are different, and difference is important. Companies are different, and therefore, the difference in each company is important and should be taken into consideration in regard to the difference within people.

This book is for you – not to sell the industry, but to give you, the reader, an honest look into the industry and the facts that you can expect may affect your business. These are facts that few people have ever considered before, let alone revealed before. Enjoy the book. Study the book. Apply the book when you look at the industry.

To you the reader: I hope this helps.

- Ryan

Dedicated to –
Rachael,
who is beautiful and well favored.

ACKNOWLEDGEMENTS

It wouldn't be fair not to acknowledge those who have helped me gain the experience that has given me so many opportunities. I have to acknowledge all of the companies I have worked for, all of the companies I have consulted for, the distributors I have helped throughout my years or in turn have helped me, and all my friends that have been the greatest sounding boards.

I also need to thank those who were willing to read and reject the ideas that were originally presented in this text, but most importantly Sallie Owen who was willing to proof read and edit the text.

Of course, most importantly, I need to thank my wife and family who have been more than patient in the time that they do not have Daddy at home. Without their support nothing that has been accomplished is possible.

TABLE OF CONTENTS

CHAPTER 1

THE INDUSTRY:
THEIR SUCCESS AND FAILURE

At-home-based businesses, particularly network marketing opportunities, are significantly valuable avenues for generating income, whether it is additional income or a main stream of revenue. As much as it is not within the purpose of this chapter to detail all of the benefits of an at home based business, it is sufficient to say that considering a network marketing opportunity isn't unwise. *At-home-based businesses* give everyone an opportunity to earn an income in proportion to the work they put into it. For some it is seen as the great mediator between the classes, the place where you get out of it exactly what you put into it (although the individual "pitching" you the opportunity probably will never use that in their presentation).

Traditionally, when venturing into a network marketing opportunity, most individuals are sold on the first presentation that is pitched to them. In this presentation, they are more than likely presented with a product or a service that they are taught the value of. Then, somewhere in the discussion, they are taught general principles of network marketing and the potential of duplication. They are also taught some vague ideas about the compensation plan model that is specific to the company they are learning about and maybe a little bit as to why this model is easier or more ethical than the next. Then, at the peak of emotion, there is an option presented for purchasing either a large pack or a small pack to begin their at-home-based business. And with that they are in.

Yet, with that, the industry claims it as a success when this takes place, but should see it as their failure more than anything else. The industry (comprising of the whole of network marketing corporations) sees it as a success because they have recruited one more person into the realm of network marketing. They got one more person to believe (as they do) that network marketing has potential and can generate a lifestyle or a product that can benefit someone's life.

The truth is that what took place is their failure more than success, because it got them close to the mark, but not close enough. Network marketing has potential, and it can change lives. There are products produced that increase longevity and total wellness that can only flow through network marketing. There are opportunities to generate wealth, gain recognition, and work from home while creating a legitimate business. The concept of network marketing can realistically create the dream – but each person's path to that dream is different and requires different things.

By having someone enroll in a company because of a sales pitch in their home might bring them into the fold, but it may not be the environment needed for personal success. Statistically speaking, three months from this sales pitch, this new home-based business owner will have a pile of product somewhere in their home, a number of friends who will not talk to them anymore, family members who will avoid them at reunions, and a total earning gross of less than twenty five dollars. At this point, these people will get frustrated, quit, and never

2

again listen to another network marketing opportunity again. The shame of this story is that they will never consider another at-home-based business because they may never consider that the one they first tried wasn't the right one for them. To borrow from a commonly known phrase, "it would be better that they had never known the industry, than to have known the industry and failed at it".

The flip side to this story is that if this individual realizes the full potential and goes to work, over time they can produce a reasonable check – something that they could be proud of. They may be paying their car payment or house payment, or even helping build a residual income for retirement. The issue that evolves here is the same as before. They joined the first opportunity that came along, even if it might not have been the right one for them. They joined what they learned first, even if the company was designed to work against their individual needs, and they built their check working against either their natural instincts or against the currant of the company.

What happens in this case is that when the opportunity appears that is perfect for them, whether it is weeks, months, or years later – they realize that they could have been working a different business model that would have fit them better. Like most leaders (whether they realize it consciously or not), they cannot duplicate their first level of success anywhere else. For this business owner to start from scratch with a different company, it is literally asking someone to burn their store-front business down and begin again. Most leaders will never make the transition to a company more fitted to their individual style (and I'm not saying that they should).

The point here is not that every person has one at-home-based business in them (whether they know it or not), but every person (unless they are a little off the wall) **only** has one at-home-based business in them. That business can either be the first opportunity that is offered to them, and they could fail, or if they are part of the elite 6% of the industry, find menial success; or they can research their opportunities and find the right company for them and increase their chance of success and their level of fulfillment.

Do your research! Learn yourself, your needs, and accept that network marketing is an option - just work on finding the right option for you. Accept that you have one real go at this, and learn what you should expect and what you should demand from your opportunity.

I am confident that at-home-based businesses are a pathway to fulfilled dreams and rewards. I have seen success throughout the industry, and I have seen failure. I have seen people grow and flourish in the right opportunities, communities, and organizations; and I have seen those same people, who once succeeded, fail by standing in the wrong place, having moved to the wrong opportunity, and no longer feeling that connection with what they are doing. I know that each of us can feel the same way that I feel about the industry.

Why am I so confident in the industry? It is not because of economic statistics, stories of grandeur, or even long-term tax benefits – even though all of the proof is out there. It is because of something more real and takes place on an individual level.

Next time you listen to someone who is trying to convince you of the potential within network marketing, I want you to pay attention to what hooks you in the conversation. Pay special attention to when and where you get excited about the opportunity. Most people are surprised when they do this, because it is usually not about selling a product, it is not about specific information on the compensation plan, or even facts about the greatness that is within the corporate staff. What excites people is the concept of the potential within network marketing. What really gets people hooked is the realization that mathematically speaking, with the power of duplication, the general concepts of networking are astounding. It is something worth getting excited about. Someone could build a check with the help of others – and have financial success.

They get hooked on the potential of network marketing! There is something within each of us that responds not to specifics about the company but to the concept of network marketing as a whole; and that says something. That says that there is something there in the concept of network marketing that is true.

We have to be careful here. Although this enlightenment on network marketing takes place often, too often the connection between the power of network marketing and the company that is being presented become false. As people receive that realization of true potential with the concept of network marketing, they mistakenly apply that excitement to the company that they learned it from; and not to sound too critical of an industry that I love – that is where they get you.

What I love about watching this industry and the behavior, both inside corporate and outside in the field, is watching why people sign up with a company. There are a number of people who will join with a company, not because of product, but because of business opportunity alone. There are very, very, very few who will join only for product. The gross majority of people join as a result of some combination of product conviction and some degree of conversion to the potential of network marketing. This means that nearly everyone who joins a network marketing company has to be convinced, not of the plan, product, or company, but to some degree of the potential in networking – otherwise not a soul would join. Network Marketing has too much of a stigma surrounding it for someone to join without some degree of conversion.

Remember that this is your at-home-based business. It is a business, and therefore, should be treated as such. There is no industry in the world that you would consider starting a business in without at least a little research behind your actions. Be aware of the industry and at least some basic concepts that can help you make your decisions when deciding where to plant your network.

Thoughts to take away from this chapter:
- Network Marketing is a viable option.
- Research to discover the best opportunity for you.
- Don't give up if your previous experiences haven't met your expectations.
- Be aware of the industry as a whole.

CHAPTER 2

YOURSELF:
NEEDS, WANTS, AND EXPECTATIONS

In identifying which network marketing opportunity is right for you, the most important step in the process is learning "YOU". An honest evaluation of your abilities and your character traits (strengths and weaknesses) can go a long way in revealing what you will need to succeed, different than what someone else might require to succeed.

Each company is different, and each organization (or upline team) offers different tools and support. Learning what your needs are in order to succeed will be critical in evaluating if a company or a sponsoring leader can support you adequately.

This takes a high degree of introspection that most people should, but don't do very often.

HONEST INTROSPECTION
Take some time and evaluate what you like to do, your hobbies, and where your time is spent. This might be work, the gym, your child's baseball games, or even working in the yard. Use this list to evaluate how many people you come in contact with. Will you come in contact with enough people to feed the needed numbers to find success (however you define it – to be

discussed later in this chapter)? Do you have enough places where you meet new people? These numbers would help you first identify if you will have enough contacts throughout your days to build in a traditional style (by word of mouth).

Then you will need to evaluate how comfortable you feel in talking with these people about an opportunity or product. Do you feel more comfortable talking to friends and family or strangers (whom you may never see again)? How do you handle face-to-face rejection? And are you more likely to quit when someone you love criticizes what you are doing, or to quit when you feel cheated by someone?

If you are the sales guy of the century, and you feel no shame in any situation when approaching someone about a product or opportunity – than you can just skip the next few paragraphs, because almost any network marketing company will be for you. If, on the other hand, you are like everyone else in the world, it is important to note what makes you feel uncomfortable about the opportunities that you may hear in the future, and what type of environment would soothe some of those concerns. Make a list of what has or does make you feel uneasy about network marketing:

- Talking to people?
- Selling a product?
- How you will be perceived by others?
- Not a comfortable people person?
- Technologically inept?
- Lack of personal network?
- Lack of personal knowledge in the industry?
- Lack of creativity or even professional experience?

Many concerns that arise in this exercise can be areas of personal growth, and can be developed. But there are some areas of personal growth, for some people, that cannot be developed comfortably for whatever reason. A little discomfort for personal growth is not a bad thing, but those areas that create a massive amount of anxiety or fear will rarely develop into a safe and enjoyable working tool. Again, be honest with yourself about what areas of discomfort could be changed with perspective and practice to improve upon yourself as a whole, or what are areas of phobias and anxiety. Once these are identified, you will have a good idea of your limitations and potentials already.

I am a large advocate that network marketing can not only generate a good deal of health and wealth in the world, but it can also (when done properly) create better, more open people. As this world becomes much more individually secluded by technology, network marketing can get people into social circumstances that can help them develop greater social skills and yield a higher quality of life (whether they ever take a check home or not). Part of learning where you are only uncomfortable and where a phobia exists is learning where the line is between the discomfort of personal growth and psychological pain. Allow your at-home-based business to give you freedom and growing experiences, and ensure that you don't risk happiness for success (because it is ultimately an unnecessary risk).

The industry is full of options, all hoping to get you interested by making these building situations more comfortable for you. For those of you who are uncomfortable on a one-on-one setting, there are party planning companies – who are more focused on getting friends together and having a good time while you are introducing them to a product. For those who may have limited opportunities to talk with people throughout the day, or know that they will blow through their warm market (friends and family) quickly without any future recruits available – there are options that are more internet-based or leaders with programs to help you find cold contacts. If you can't face rejection or are terrified to talk with people about things related to this industry, there are still options for you in the industry – they just require a little more attention from your sponsoring team. In a case like that, you will want someone to help you and be your third party – so that you have someone else to talk about the product or opportunity when you find someone.

YOUR ABILITIES

Learning about yourself and your limitations with a strong degree of honesty will actually help you learn exactly what you need from your company and your sponsoring organization. You will want to make sure that they are going to be able to accommodate your limitations. Equally important in this process, you should look at your abilities, and see what you do bring to the table. Evaluate the unique opportunities that you do have, and what you will be adding to the team. You might not be able to talk with someone openly about the product or to stand in front of a large crowd and teach about the opportunity, but you may be able to introduce your team members to a population of people who they otherwise wouldn't be able to meet. You may have contacts in the business community, sport teams, or local celebrities who can add clout and caliber to your product and the program of your team.

There are unlimited possibilities, because everyone brings something unique and valuable to the team. The value is seen in indentifying those strengths in yourself and in others and maximizing them.

- Do you have specific technical skills?
- Do you know how to help build a team website or maximize search engine optimization?
- Do you have contacts in the food or service industry of the product you would be selling or talking about?

- Do you have a degree or education in something related to the product or company?
- Do you carry with you some clout or standing in society or the people you mingle with?
- Do you have good communication skills, or do some people just like you easily?

There are unlimited options, gifts, and talents that you and others bring to a team, many of which could never be detailed sufficiently in a book like this. Be aware that they are there, and be creative in discovering them; and be just as creative in using those talents in your business. Network Marketing can be one of the greatest self-discovery experiences you may ever experience.

The key in your evaluation has a lot to do with honestly knowing your limitations and finding the right team and corporation for your needs, as well as openly knowing what you can bring to the table. Everyone has something that someone else doesn't have. Everyone knows someone that someone else doesn't know (that is the value that everyone brings – their own personal network of relationships). Everyone has a skill that someone else doesn't have. What is yours? Know it, embrace it, and love it. Work it to your success.

DEFINE SUCCESS AND GOALS

In knowing what your personal needs are, you also need to understand what you require to get out of the program before you consider yourself successful. Identify what success is to you in that process – and be realistic about it. Success is, and should be, different for each person. This is where identifying your needs, wants, and managing your expectations merges all into one.

A discussion on the following questions should help conform your needs, wants, and expectations to your potential:
- Do you have realistic expectations?
- What is your definition of success?
- What do you *want* out of the program?
- What do you *need* (as minimum requirements) out of the program?

Do you have realistic expectations?

Many people are first introduced or even "converted" to the network marketing industry by hearing of huge checks with easy attempts. They hear that someone made over $100,000 last year and was only doing it part time, or that someone else made over a million dollars in their first three months just by doing something simple. They see and hear big numbers and are convinced that it is possible.

There are a few things that you should know about these situations.

THE WORKER, THE WORKED, AND THE ACCIDENTS

It is possible for someone to make big money, and it really does happen in the industry. There are people who are making a good deal of money on a monthly and weekly basis. With that said, you should also understand that these people normally fall into one of two categories: "the worker" or "the worked".

The people who are making big money in the industry make it their lives, and they work hard at it. These are the people you can spot in a crowd, because they are good at what they do, and they do it all the time. They draw people to them, are charismatic, and are always "on". These are "the workers", and they earn every penny that they get.

12

"The Worked", on the other hand, are the lucky ones or the unique cases you hear about. These are people who happen to have some physical, mental, or financial handicap, but then are able to find success "because of the ease of the program".

These stories of the lucky are usually created by the company, glorified, or even exaggerated. Often times, they are made by the company – that is why we title them "the worked". It will be true that they are earning a fat check from an awesome organization, but usually this is because someone else built that organization. Someone else saw the benefit for themselves (whether it was corporate or a sponsoring business owner) of building this poor blind ladies organization.

The reason they do this is to appeal to your sense of competition and ease. They want you to look at someone and think, "if they can do it being poor, handicapped, and uneducated – than I sure can". Often times, they will play to your prejudices and your sense of competition. Some claim that they do it to inspire you, which may be true in some circumstances, but either way they do it to get you in.

With that said, the point of this discussion isn't to make you see the industry for what it is – it is to help you identify the stories that you are hearing, and be able to adjust appropriately to the hype. Too many people fall into these stories, increase the expectations to an unrealistic level, and then become disappointed and disenfranchised with network marketing. The network marketing industry is what it is, just like every other industry in the world. This is intended to help you understand that there is no free money – and there is no easy way to riches (not even in network marketing).

There is a third category of stories that you will hear earning big money, and although they are more rare than either 'the workers" or "the worked" they are just as disproportionately advertised. These are "the accidents". These are people who just happen to be at the right place, at the right time, and sign up just the right people. They have applied themselves only minimally to the program and are bringing home a significant additional income. These are accidents in every sense of the word, are extremely rare, and could never be duplicated. Yet, this is what we all hope for when we first enroll in a network marketing company, as unrealistic as it is.

By the time you start to hear the stories of BIG money coming from "the worked", or you start to hear the story of a blind lady in the middle of Iowa who is making 100k a year – the time to make easy money as an accident has already passed (if it was ever there to begin with). Very few people will ever luck out and fall into easy money in network marketing – but there are a disproportionate amount of stories about it. And it will never happen twice in the same company.

EQUAL REACTION

The first thing that I ask people when they ask me about how to find success in the industry is, "What are your expectations, and are they realistic?"

If you answer that question with "big money", I would respond that it is perfectly possible, but "what are your expectations of time, effort, and work?" That is where people blink for a moment.

Remember what we learned in grade school about Newton's 3rd Law of Gravity, and realize that it can be applied to just about every facet of life. Every result is an equal reaction to the force put behind it.

There are great options and opportunities to make a significant income in the network marketing world. But your expectations need to be realistic and correct for your goals and abilities. Like anything in the world, what you get out will be in proportion to what you put in. I counsel everyone that I have ever spoken to about making money in the industry, "if you want full-time pay, you need to put full-time effort into it; part-time pay, part-time effort." Just be aware of that; be aware of what you can put into it, so that you can be aware of what you should expect to get out of it.

If you want to fly around in a private jet and make a seven-figure income, then you better be the best at it, and you better be willing to put your best effort into it.

If you want a full-time paycheck from it, then you should be ready to study and prepare and work as if it were your full-time job.

If you want a part-time paycheck from it, then you should be willing to commit that time to it.

Realize that network marketing is the perfect form of labor work (and occasionally more rewarding). You get out of it what you put into it. That is its beauty. Anyone who works their trash off in a traditional job will only get paid what they have contracted for (often whether they work hard or not); but anyone who works over-time in network marketing will see that extra time reflected in their check. Everyone is on the same level and starts with the same opportunity.

Having your expectations in check, with a realistic outlook, can be the difference in finding success when others find disappointment. Make your expectations realistic and your work ethic conform, and if you happen to be one of the lucky ones – then you will just be that much more successful.

What is your definition of success?

Do you need to make a million dollars, or do you need to pay off your car? What level of success, earnings, or recognition do you feel will justify your working your at-home-based business ? More importantly, at what point would you no longer be ashamed of being a network marketer?

Know these answers, and these are your goals.

Some people need full-time pay, and that is success. It would change many people's lives if they could have their house payment, or even their car payment, paid with their business earnings. There are great people and great marketers who love the product so much that they find a great deal of success in just being able to pay for their own product or are getting it for free. These are great stepping stones of success. By identifying them, and marking them as successful, you will have a much greater sense of well-being in the process, and be fulfilled much sooner. These are all levels of success.

Write down your definition of success, and have more than one. Put them somewhere that you will see them whenever you sit down to evaluate how your business is going. Make it a list of levels of success. For example:

- Pay for your product with your commission earnings
- Pay for your marketing or business investment costs
- Pay your car payment
- Pay off your credit cards
- Pay your house payment
- Start paying down principle on your loans
- Get out of debt entirely
- Month long trip backpacking through Europe where you bring your favorite network marketing author with you

Make a stepping stone list of success, whatever it may include (or not include if Europe is not your thing), and then rejoice and be proud when you hit these milestones of success.

Without these milestones of success set on paper and checked regularly, it is easy to get discouraged and only see where you are not, instead of where you have come from and how far you have gone. By placing only one goal, "Millionaire", on your mirror – will you just be discouraged that is hasn't worked out, even if you are a making full-time pay? By creating stepping stone goals, and defining your own success, you will be more likely to achieve all your goals, and be more fulfilled throughout the process.

What do you want out of the program?
Some of you might sense that this area is a little redundant; because most people think what they all want is money and good product. The reality is that most people, whether they know it or not, want much more from this industry – and for some that is the driving reason they join.

Here is another moment of sheer honest introspection:
- Do you expect to gain friends in the process?
- To become acquainted with a larger community of people?
- To hold parties and have a good time occasionally?
- To have somewhere to go besides church and work?
- Maybe find a hobby?
- What else are you looking for from this opportunity?

I will tell you that you can find it in network marketing, but you have to know you are looking for it – because just like everything else, you will need to work for it and join the right opportunity that will give you exactly what you are looking for. How can you find what you want if you do not know what you are looking for?

What do you need to get out of the program?

Out of all of this, you need to know exactly what you will need to get out of the program to justify your even starting. Document all that we have detailed above, but also document what you need to even start.

How much money do you need to get in your first month to justify spending what you are spending? What will you need to justify the time that will be necessary to get things going?

Do this so that you are again aware of what you will need to achieve and in what time frame. As you go through the process of selecting a program, you will want to have this information available and compare this need (along with all of the other topics detailed in this chapter) with the program, and determine if there is a direct and detailed path to your success with whatever program you choose.

You may even choose to share this information with those who are trying to sponsor you to a company. By starting your working relationship with honesty and openness, you can help them understand what your needs are, and begin the process of helping them help you. Be honest, and tell them how much you need to make, in what time frame, to make it worth your time, or what kind of activity you will need to justify taking your time away from something else (family, friends, other employment opportunities). What this allows you to do is create an open relationship of expectations with the person or team sponsoring you and you are able to discuss the possibilities of finding those needs with them or with the company.

In a best case scenario, you and your sponsor should sit down from the very beginning and map out how these needs are going to be met through their program and the company's compensation plan. If you can walk away from one of your first meetings feeling comfortable that you now know how to fulfill your needs, in what time frame, and what is expected from you in the process, you have a good sign that you might be with the right sponsor and company.

APPLICATION: TOP OF THE TREE FALLACY

One example that can be applied with the level of honesty that is being discussed comes from the "Top of the Tree Fallacy". This is one area where you can see that being honest about your needs, wants, expectations, and abilities can affect your placement or team choosing.

In network marketing there is a common term used, "Top of the Tree". This means that their account or business position in the company organization is at or near the top of the structural tree. What this also implies is that the rest of the company is somewhere under them, and therefore, they have a large amount of volume under them. As a result, the implication also extends that because everyone or most of the company organization is under their business that they are earning a significant amount as a result. This isn't always the case, and when developing compensation plans, corporations usually make sure that just because you have a huge group under you (even if you are at the top of the tree), that you don't walk away with millions unless you have actually built or developed it (a.k.a. are a worker).

Yet, with this term comes a lot of excitement. Many times as people start to build with a newer company, they will use the term "top of the tree" to try and convince you that you will have some great advantage. Indeed, being at the top of a built tree does have its advantages, but the truth of the matter is, enrolling at the top of the tree doesn't mean that things will be handed to you – and you will need to be aware of that and adjust your expectations accordingly.

Many times, what people don't consider when they hear the term "top of the tree' is what type of help they will be getting as a result, or in exchange for, that top of the tree placement. People assume that because they are near the top of the tree, they will get some free help from the company – because after all, people will need to be placed somewhere and why not under you. This can be true, but not always. Having worked in a corporate setting within network marketing companies my whole career, I am aware that corporate teams don't just give people and teams to distributors or business owners because they are at the top of the tree. They give teams and references to people who are working, regardless of placements. Also, even if a team is built for you, that doesn't mean that you will be paid on it until you engage and go to work (this of course takes into consideration the type of compensation plan).

What you do trade for being near the top of the tree, for the help from corporate which may or may not come, is upline support. The closer you are to the top of the tree, the fewer people you have to call on for aid. Because you would be near the top of the tree, you may only have a small handful of people who would be interested in your success, and many of them will have whole teams to choose from helping. Whereas, if you had chosen to go lower in the tree, under a number of leaders who were already built and were still engaged in the company, you would have untold numbers of people you could contact to get aid and support from.

This means that, unlike the common perception that is given to being at the "top of the tree", the closer you are to the top of the tree – the more self motivated you will need to be, and the less you will need to rely on any aid or help. If you are the type of person that really can build a business on their own, then the top of the tree might be a good spot for you. If you are like the rest of us, and need training and support to help build your group – realize that fact, and avoid the hype that goes with being at the top of the tree.

I mention this fallacy just as an example of something that someone can develop a good degree of excitement around, but may not necessarily be the best for you in the long run. There are a number of these in network marketing, whether it is the Top of the Tree Fallacy, the story of the accident earner, or some other gimmick. Now that they are out there, be aware that when you are feeling hype about something, it usually is something that won't apply to you in your circumstances.

Some will hate me in writing this, because it appears as if I am trying to take the excitement out of the industry, which I am not. My experience has shown that the people who have the greatest experience and earning potential in the industry are excited with realistic expectations and a solid work ethic. If someone works towards a false story with easy expectations, no matter how hard they work, they will not be able to achieve what has been promised or expected, because it is not realistic.

EXAMPLE

Many years ago, as I was working for a newer company that was trying to get off the ground, I witnessed where the concepts of "The Worked", the Top of the Tree Fallacy, and the eventual honesty of the distributor came full circle.

As this small company was trying to get off the ground, it chose as part of its marketing, the idea of making a success story. There was a young man, newly married, who had just started his college education that had enrolled in the company. Unknown to him, he was chosen to be their man. The company then placed all of their contacts and all of their own potential leaders under this young man, and he was placed at the top of the tree.

This was a boy who had never done network marketing before, and really didn't know what he was doing – and it showed. But that was what they were looking for. Eventually he dropped out of his schooling as he saw his check increase, and they began to take pictures of him and his checks and publish them online and throughout different publications. He began to speak at meetings, and to share some of his great experience through company-sponsored presentations. Needless to say, this experience was false, and although he believed he had accomplished something great, we all knew that he was made by the company, and was one of "the worked" by all definitions.

In looking back, it worked in all contexts, because I think people even saw through him when he spoke. He didn't have any real experience recruiting, or selling, or even an understanding of basic network marketing concepts that could be realistically applied. People looked at him and said, "If he could do it, than I can do it". And the company was happy because they had a success story that made them look successful.

Of course, his ego got larger and larger, and part of a corporate job is to put up with the monster that they had created. They dealt with it, and let him speak whenever he wanted – and made sure that they made him feel confident with his success.

Then one day, just at the brink of having financial security for the future of the company (just at the break even marker), their financial backing backed out. Apparently, the principle investor didn't have the money they claimed to, and it appeared that the company was either going to be shutting its doors or be forced into a merger. In a short while, they started the merging process with another company and an entirely different structured compensation plan.

At the conclusion of the merger, this young man still had most (if not all) of his previous organization, but because it was a forced success, when they merged him into this new plan, his check dropped to almost nothing.

Here was our biggest leader, and our biggest earner. One year making six figures and putting in minimal work, and the next barely making part-time pay from it. The company did everything they could to help his check, but it was helpless. What they had done had just become extremely transparent; eventually he was seen for what he was.

This was the moment of truth for this young man. Within a few months, he realized how benefited he was in his previous position. He realized just how much help he had been given from corporate, and how much help he wasn't going to be getting from them now that they had a much larger organization to manage. He also quickly realized how much it didn't help him to be at the top of the tree. He had no one to go to in order to help him grow or get the training that was necessary and that he needed so badly. His team had more experienced members than he was, and there were times when he wished he was placed further down in his own organization than at the top.

At this moment, he had to make a choice. He could have either given up and cursed the circumstances which gave him success and then took it away, or he could engage and start to build a business. He took some time and evaluated his wants, needs, and his expectations. He re-evaluated what his perception of himself was, and no longer considered himself as a "top of the tree" player, even though that was his location. He started to work and developed a program for himself. He lived close to the corporate office, and would invite people to come for a tour of the office, and then teach them about the product and opportunity. That was something that he could do and was within his abilities.

I saw him in the office every single day, and often times, he was even there longer than I was. He wanted full-time pay, and he put full-time effort into it.

He built his business – and went from being made by the company, to helping to make the company.

Each situation is different, and each person has different needs. We all have different abilities, and wants. Taking time to honestly evaluate ourselves, our wants, needs and expectations can help us choose an appropriate opportunity, and can be the difference between frustration and success.

Thoughts to take away from this chapter:
- Take time to have honest introspection on your needs, wants and expectations.
- Define what your success is going to be.
- Get stepping stone goals and keep them where you can see your continued growth.
- Be aware of the stories you hear and adjust your expectations appropriately.
- Identify what you are willing to put into the program in accordance with what you want.

CHAPTER 3

YOUR SPONSOR:
TEAM, TOOLS, SUCCESS, AND SUPPORT

If it isn't already defined for you, your sponsor is usually identified as the person who introduced you to the opportunity. This is the person that is being compensated with a portion of your own success, and therefore, is expected to help support you in this process. You are considered to be in their downline, and they are your upline. The organization that you are a part of is the complete team of upline sponsors who are all benefiting from each other's success, and therefore, should be seen as a team or support group. These are a few terms of the industry that I am sure you will pick up shortly as you begin your endeavor. These are people that you have the option to be working with.

Admittedly, this should be the chapter that you spend the least amount of time in, because this is the one topic that you will have the least control over. You can, and should, do all of your due diligence to go through this chapter and learn all that you can about the person or team you will be working with and the organization that you are a part of. With that said, you should also realize that you should not completely rely on your organization or your team for your success. You can expect them to help you and support you, and you should hope for that.

You should select a team that you feel comfortable will help you as much as possible, but when you begin, please realize that your success will be based on your actions and your involvement in your business – not someone else's actions. You are ultimately responsible for your own success.

One reason that this contradictory concept is present (learn who will help you the most, but don't rely on it), is because you can never really know until you are involved just how much someone is going to help and support your organization. They can talk the talk, and promise the world, but when it comes time to deliver, may even fall short of their own expectations. Indeed, it is within their best interest to help and support your team, because as your team grows, so does theirs – but that is not to say that they even know how to support properly, or that your definition of support and their definition of support are the same thing. Your sponsor or team may be supporting you in their minds eye, but because you may need something else to help grow your abilities, you may feel left without support.

BEING WORTHY OF SUPPORT

There is another key in this. As a sponsor, it is much easier to support, encourage, and help people who are going about and trying to help themselves. In fact, when I meet with people who are doing a great job recruiting and are in a position to help build someone, I strongly encourage them not to help build anyone who hasn't already helped to build themselves – who isn't showing a little bit of self motivation. This is because the new recruit that is placed under someone who hasn't built anything is the one that is taking the risk; here they are being placed with an upline that may, or may not, be there next week, and it is ultimately not fair to them. If the upline that the new recruit is placed under doesn't show enough motivation to start his own business, how can you expect him to properly support, encourage, and mentor the new business owner.

In this light, I strongly encourage you to be a self motivator and to grow your team and organization as much as you can, regardless of what your upline or sponsor can, or will, do for you. You will be surprised as you grow how many people will come out of the woodwork to help you grow, when you are trying to grow it yourself. Those who work hard themselves usually find a much stronger level of support from upline and even from corporate.

Learn what your sponsor and upline organization can help you with, and then go forward as if you do not expect any support.

LEARN YOUR UPLINE TEAM

Know your team, who you are going to be working with, and who you will have available at your disposal. Learn about your sponsor's upline. Try to answer as many of these questions as possible:

- Who is in your upline (who will be affected positively by your success)?
- Who can you connect with among them?
- How successful has your sponsor and upline been in network marketing in the past?
- How successful has your sponsor and upline been in any previous industries in the past?
- How successful have the leaders been in this current opportunity?
- How successful has your sponsor been in this current opportunity?
- Can you get along with your sponsor (as well as any upline that you may be connecting or working with)?

- What kind of programs or tools does the organization or team offer that may be different from another team of upline?

Who is in your upline (who will be affected positively by your success)?

When speaking to your potential sponsor, try to identify with those who constitute your upline team. These are considered people who sponsored your sponsor, and who sponsored them, and so on, all the way up to the top of the tree. Identify as many people in this line that will be invested or interested in your success, because you will be in their team.

Try to identify ranks or levels of success within the current compensation plan, and see at which point in your upline the incentive to help you stops. This incentive wall will happen for a number of reasons. Sometimes upline loses incentive just because you are so far down, or even because there is already ample support between you and them. By identifying where your potential support stops is important, because that will help you see who realistically is incentivized to help you grow.

This entire line of people, from you up to the last leader who benefits from your success, is going to be considered your upline team and your potential support. Know how many people are there, and try to get names and general locations, and get to know as much about all of them as possible.

In this process, do not get discouraged if there is an overwhelming amount of "nobodies" or half-engaged people, just be focused on finding those who are real leaders and would be in a real position to help you. Sometimes, this list of potential support can be as long as fifty people, but unfortunately, most of them do not have the foresight or the conviction to really dig down in their group and help you grow – even when it is within their best interests. This is ultimately okay as long as you can find within those fifty people, two or three who are determined and self-actualized within the organization. These are people with the foresight to see that team work increases duplication, support and profits.

Make a list and be sure to contact them, and get an idea about who they are both by reputation and by person. The upline who is indifferent to your call is not interested in really building their business or yours. The upline who gains a good degree of excitement will be there for at least some degree of success. The upline that begins to work out a plan of action to help you build your business, offers you support in your meetings, or helping your team – is the catch.

Who can you connect with among them?

In the best case scenario you will need to know who you can connect with for more advanced support. By connecting, I refer to being able to contact them for three-way phone calls, third-party validation, general support for your team, and for advanced advice. In realistic terms, the more people you can connect with, the more people you can have supporting you, and the more likely you will have success. By connecting and working with a number of people through your upline (particularly leaders of your group), your experience will increase much quicker, and your team will mature to a higher level. By getting support from a number of different avenues, you will be able to more effectively cherry pick your own personal style and have more models of success to base your activity on. This is just more support for you, and each one will carry with them their own skills and abilities that can help you grow. Know your upline, and use them as you try to build your business. By knowing who you are working with above you, you can more effectively connect your recruits to likeminded upline, giving everyone a greater sense of security, team unity, and completeness.

In the worst case scenario, you will need to know who you can connect with should your immediate sponsor fail you. You need to learn who you can contact to get additional training, direction and support from people who will also be benefited by your success. The reality is that you will always have your sponsor fail you at one time or another. It is sad to say, but it is inevitable. That is not to say that they will not be able to support you from that point on, but no one is perfect (all the time), not even your sponsor. Be aware of this, be prepared for this, and don't be overly offended when this happens. People have lives, and so should you – and you, more than likely, will fail your downline sometime throughout your career.

If, in the case of your network marketing experience, your direct sponsor goes inactive, loses the vision, or leaves the company, please do not get discouraged by this. This is one important reason why it is so important to identify who you can connect with and get that support that your sponsor is neglecting. Jump your direct communication right above him to the next upline contact. They will be aware that your sponsor has become a blank spot, and they are being affected negatively by that. They will want to save your activity and work with you in an effort not to lose any more of their team as a result.

How successful has your sponsor and upline been in network marketing in the past?

This should be broken down into separate concepts between your sponsor and the upline.

Does your sponsor have any experience in past network marketing? Have they had any success themselves? If not, that is not necessarily a problem; the key is being aware that this is the circumstance. If you are dealing with a sponsor that does not have any experience, be aware that they may surprise themselves and not enjoy the business as much as they thought. In these circumstances, you need to be aware that there is always a possibility that they might no longer be there next month.

Even more importantly, this is good to keep in mind when they do not offer you the support that you need, or thought they could provide. Don't take it personally, but understand that they are currently on a learning curve themselves. This learning curve also means that there is good potential in that you may not need to take everything they tell you about the industry as gospel truth. They themselves might not fully understand what they are talking about.

On the other hand, if you have a direct sponsor who has had some experience, this is a great resource, as you know that they have a little understanding of what it takes to be successful. Try to identify what level of success they have had, even if it is menial, because any level of success shows that they at least have some concept of what lies ahead on the road and the work it will take. This is also important, as long as we remember the concept that most people will only be as good as the person teaching them (in any subject). If your sponsor has had a level of success that you wish to exceed, realize that you will then need to go above this person to gain greater training.

This means that you will also need to know your upline and the success that they have had in the industry previous to the current opportunity. Have they been a big leader in another company, and if so, what was their degree of success? Knowing this information can really help to identify who you can go to when you need further training and advice beyond what your close network of people can supply.

IDENTIFYING THE REAL LEADER

If you can identify upline who have accomplished something significant in more than one company, this is a two edged sword.

Most leaders in the industry are confident that everything they have been able to accomplish is a result of their efforts. These leaders neglect the fact that most of their business success usually comes from some combination of hard work and good luck. They have enrolled the right person, at the right time, to build the right team, and freed up their own time to start building elsewhere in their organization. When leaders don't see that they are the product of both work ethic and some type of divine providence, they sometimes can be neglectful of the intangible that has made them a success. When they jump to a new network marketing company, it becomes a moment of truth, and although they are extremely confident that the same level of success can happen twice for them, it is rarely the case. This can be discouraging to them; but nevertheless, when there is a history of success at least you know that they have some concept of what is involved in building a company and organization, more so than someone who has never had success.

Yet, when those rare times come that someone has had success in more than one company, there is a much greater chance that these are real leaders. Real leaders are those who do not have success following them (like most leaders assume), but those that make success. They are able to build something out of nothing because they know how to utilize luck and still build despite the lack of it. These are rare to find, but when they are found, they are sure to build success as long as they are committed.

The two-edge sword appears in the fact that they have found success in MORE than one company. This usually means that they have jumped ship from one company to the next for one reason or another; and there is a chance that they will do the same thing with the current opportunity. They may build a great business and then just jump to the next business. When identifying a potential candidate for jumping ship, it is important to try to get as much information about them as possible, and learn how they have treated their previous companies and organizations.

Some will only jump if they can ensure that they will never jeopardize their previous organizations. These are good leaders who, when they move, will not try to jeopardize their checks by getting in legal problems through trying to take teams with them to the new organization or company. If this is the case your only concern is to try to learn as much from them as possible and create as much of a team as you can in the time (few years) that the company holds their interest.

There are others that you will want to keep an eye on. When they jump to new companies, they try to take as many people with them as possible. This can decimate your organization if this happens; particularly if they had been helping you build your team. Granted, there are legal policies against this happening in every company, but even the attempt (as unsuccessful as it might be) can create a great deal of disunity with a team, and ultimately threaten your check and organization.

Learn what level of success everyone has had and the type of leaders you are planning on working with. Changing peoples' personalitities and styles are not usually an option when discussing upline – but being aware and preparing for the potential realities can be invaluable and wise.

How successful has your sponsor and upline been in any previous industries in the past?

This is particularly important if there is limited experience in your upline organization or sponsor. The reason I ask this is that it can sometimes be a sign of how dedicated and successful they can be in network marketing. Successful people usually hang out with successful people, and they usually take great pride in being as successful as they are.

Although not an exact science, and not always the best gauge of their level of success in network marketing, it can at least give you an idea of what they are willing to put forward in trying to become a success in their new endeavor. Some people are just successful in everything they do, because that is part of whom they accept themselves to be; while others always fail because that is what they expect themselves to be. There is a happy medium of people that fit somewhere in between – but it is at least something I think is worth considering.

Look at how many successes these people have had outside of network marketing, and identify if they are in good social arenas that demand self-motivation. Real estate, entrepreneur, small business owner, or any other similar areas that demand someone to literally get in the dirt and build are great success stories that say a lot about someone's potential to work in network marketing.

But with this, you also need to look at how many failures someone has had as well.

In many respects, you are trying to look at their personality for perseverance, persistence, and stubbornness towards success.

How successful have the leaders been in this current opportunity?

Every opportunity is different, and I am always surprised by who can and cannot succeed in different environments and organizations. Cultures and building strategies change from company to company. Many times, big leaders from one organization that move to another learn this lesson, and very few of them are able to duplicate the same level of success a second time.

As discussed earlier, real leaders are able to duplicate themselves, regardless of the culture or circumstances. With this information, you should be aware that just because someone was successful in another company doesn't mean that they will have the same level of success in the new opportunity. Know what ranks they have achieved since they have moved to the new company (if this is a new company for them) and how much they are making. Most big leaders in the industry are a combination of hard work and luck – and sadly luck doesn't strike twice. Real leaders are successful despite luck, and will succeed whether it strikes or not – these are few and far between (less than .1% of the industry, and maybe even less). There is nothing worse than being in the organization of a former big leader from another company who jumps ship to a new opportunity only to get discouraged when he learns that he wasn't the hot-shot that he thought he was – eventually they all stop working and just collect the check (whatever check might be there).

Identify the most successful people in the organization and cling to them. Learn all you can from them and their experience, and see how you can help to apply your abilities to their organization (through the building of your organization).

How successful has your sponsor been in the current opportunity?

Your sponsor doesn't need to be a big hitter in order to gauge the potential with the company. An easy question to ask anyone who is talking to you about making money is: How much money have you made?

This is a critical question, and can really open up a great deal of information. If the sponsor is telling you how easy it is to earn your first thousand dollars, ask them whether they have earned that amount using the same program. If not, then find out why they haven't had success.

Your direct sponsor doesn't need to make the money you hope to make or even enough to pay for their car payment, but they should make enough to make them satisfied with the program. Remember that you should not limit yourself to what they make, but you can use what they make as a gauge of ease and potential. If you know your sponsor well enough, and you know that they are hard-working people with solid determination, and they have had little to no success to date – there might be something you or they are missing in the program. If you know them to only do easy things, and are finding that they are hitting their goals, but could have exceeded them if they only had some decent motivation, then you can have the confidence that you can succeed and exceed their expectations for themselves. In between these two scenarios are countless options that couldn't be detailed in a text such as this, but by asking these questions, it can either increase you comfort level or solidify your discomfort.

Can you get along with your sponsor (as well as any upline that you may be connecting or working with)?

You need your sponsor to be your advocate with your new experience. You need to feel comfortable expressing your concerns to them, without them getting freaked out themselves. Best situations are when the new distributor can feel confident and comfortable with the person that they will be working with. Do not sign up with anyone that you wouldn't want to have over for dinner. If you don't like the person's attitude, then you will not succeed in the company. Regardless of how much we try to control our psychological behavior from acting irrational at times, this industry will entirely bring out all of the skeletons in the closet. If you cannot get along with your sponsor and at least feel some level of respect for them, you will have trouble building your business. If you like the company, but cannot stand you sponsor or upline, than find someone else in the company; there are other options within the same company and even organization. But this is only an option before you officially enroll.

UPLINE CLOSE DOWN

I have seen great network marketers close up shop all because they do not want to be successful and help their sponsor build his own check. Whether it is true or not, the perception is always there that your success equals their success. This is not always the case, but the concern still arises more often than not.

Many cannot get past the fact that the harder they work the more the person above them could make. If you or someone you know is in a similar situation, then get over it. This happens and it is going to happen below you as well – that is the nature of the beast. Forget about what is happening above you and just work on what you can control and your own success.

If you are not in this situation, than avoid it at all costs. Join the company you choose, with someone that you can work with, play with, get upset with, and mend bridges with. An organization should be a support group in all aspects of the definition.

What kind of programs or tools do the organization or team offer that may be different from another team or upline?

Every organization, whether it is developed by corporate staff or by an upline sponsor, should have a model of duplication. This may be a program or a tool that they offer that has been successful in selling or recruiting to that particular business. Pretty much, this is learning how they grow their business.

- Do they do meetings every Thursday night at the local school?
- Do they do three-way calls with other upline members?
- Do they do company contacting?

Ask the question to your sponsor and your upline: How do you build your business? The clearer that process is, the easier time you will have learning if that process is something that you yourself could duplicate and find similar success with.

Please note that different business owners selling the same product may have entirely different programs. You may find someone in the same company that does things differently than someone else with just as good or greater success; or you may even be able to take the reins and develop something yourself, a system for you. There is no perfect system for duplication throughout the industry. If there were, then everyone would be doing the exact same thing. But there is a good system out there for you, and a different system out there for someone else. You might thrive in front of a crowd, or be better over the phone, or be able to naturally network and support through the local PTA. Systems and programs should be easy to understand, simple to implement, and should stretch you just enough to feel like you are growing as a person, without tearing you apart.

The key to this chapter is to learn as much as you can about the people you are going to be working with. Consider these people your co-workers and your support group. Feel comfortable with them, and your experience will be a pleasure as you go through the process of building your business.

THE INTANGIBLE ANSWER

These types of questions concerning evaluating your sponsor and your upline team do not necessarily have any right answers. There is no perfect grade or multiple choice quiz that can analyze the answers to these questions and tell you whether it is a good team or not.

This is one of the reasons why I cautioned that this might be the chapter you spend the least time reviewing. As much as these are all critical questions to ask, whether they are answered correctly or not, the main concern is what is really going to happen when the rubber hits the pavement – and that is as unpredictable as the roulette table.

The main reason I request that these questions are asked is to get a greater, more realistic sense of the industry and the opportunity that is being presented. I call this the intangible answer – because it is something that is not quantitative, but is extremely qualitative. If you can listen to all these answers, prepare yourself for the work that is ahead of you, wade through all the hype, and still be genuinely excited about the people you will be working with, then there is a greater chance of finding success within this opportunity.

CAUTION OF HONESTY

I implore you at the conclusion of this chapter to be honest with your sponsor as you go through this process, and be honest with yourself. There is nothing more telling about people than how they behave in a network marketing environment.

If, at the conclusion of this chapter or book, you identify that you just cannot get along with your sponsor, let them know that you are looking for someone else to help assist you. More than likely, they wouldn't want to work with someone that didn't like them.

If, at the conclusion of this chapter or book, you identify that you will be working with, or wanting to work with, a leader further up in the organizational structure, be sure that you still enroll with your first sponsor. Don't seek out being the closest to the biggest and baddest in the organization. Work with whomever you want when you get into the business, but as much as possible, give credit where credit is due. If one person introduces you to a company and you love it, if you can, you need to stay loyal to them and allow them to get the credit for introducing you to the company. This is the basic principle of network marketing.

Thoughts to take away from this chapter:
- Be aware of your upline
- Be worthy of their support
- Learn about your sponsor and upline successes and failures
- Know who you can work with
- Know who you want to be working with
- Like the people you are going to be working with

CHAPTER 4

THE PRODUCT:
COMFORT, CONVICTION, AND CONFIDENCE

Every network marketing company has a product or service, and if it is not the case, then you are dealing with a pyramid scheme, and it should never be considered for a home based business. Arguably, the product is the single most important aspect of your at-home-based business. This would make sense, because the product or service provided is usually the most important aspect of any business. For many, the product is paramount, and not only helps you feel comfortable with what you are buying, but also with what you are selling or sharing. Your level of comfort and confidence in what you are doing is critical to your well-being, and your well-being, in any aspect of your life, is critical to your success.

COMFORT IN THE PRODUCT

One of the strongest difficulties within the industry is helping people feel comfortable with what they are doing. This is because most people do not feel confident with the idea of selling anything to anyone. Most people know how much no one likes to be "sold" anything, yet we all love to buy. In this industry, most new associates assume that this is an industry of selling instead of sharing.

This also doesn't take into account that the industry itself is self-focused on the idea of "selling". Corporate companies try to brand their industry as "Direct Selling", and compensation plans are labeled as "Commission Plans". These industry-standard terms do not aid the industry in soothing the mind of the new associate uncomfortable with the idea of "selling"; nor is it fair to display such an inaccurate portrayal of the industry where a gross number of the most successful top earners have learned that success is found in *sharing* instead of "selling".

Nevertheless, the stigma and discomfort with "selling" in the network marketing industry is present, and the most powerful tool against that disease is a good product that someone can get behind and talk about – either out of experience or pure excitement. This is a powerful reason why product is paramount in the process of selecting a network marketing company. The more confident you are about the product and what you are sharing, the more likely you will share the product with those you come in contact with. You will also feel a greater sense of satisfaction when you share it and someone reciprocates with appreciation and also enjoys the product as much as you. Without this confidence and comfort, even with financial success, you are less likely to feel the well-being in the distribution of the product you are "selling" (because that is what you are doing if you don't care about the product - selling) rather than if you were sharing something you really were happy with.

THE PRODUCT CONVICTION TRAP

Now to some degree, all of what has been said so far in this chapter goes without saying. In fact, there is something inside each of us that yearns to feel good about what they are sharing, and their psyche requires that this merger between *action* and *comfort* takes place. This merge often times happens pre-maturely and becomes a matter of false conviction to a product out of psychological necessity. This is not to say that you develop a conviction for something that is false, it may very well be a great product; it is saying that you gained your conviction not out of conversion, but out of need – and this sometimes can be damaging. If you are driving in fog, you can still be on the right road, it is just harder to tell if you are still going in the right direction and can be dangerous. Conviction can be this fog in network marketing.

As described in a previous chapter, many people find themselves committed to a network marketing company, not because of the company, but because they are converted to the potential in network marketing (as whole) and the company was the first one present at the time such conversion took place. Many people sign on the dotted line before ever tasting the product, probing their sponsors, looking over the compensation plan, or a number of other things that they may need to do. Within a few short hours, an individual has now committed themselves, often times financially (which for many is the strongest level of commitment they will express in their lives), to a company and product that they are not necessarily aware of. At this junction, when the subconscious realizes that the whole thought process has been circumvented in this "enrollment process" (that is not to say it was a mistake), the mind and psyche begin to work together to aid in the justification of such actions.

The first thing the new enrollee will do is gain an entirely unsound bias in the product or service that they are now representing. They begin to do research, absorbing every piece of positive literature, and disregarding every questionable bit of material. Often times, they find themselves totally committed to the product even before their first shipment arrives. There are even many times when the sponsor will encourage such actions with the encouragement to engage in sharing activities as soon as possible, even before that first product arrives.

All of this can take place in a matter of hours or days – but sure enough, it takes place. These actions yield a strong level of conviction in the product, but not conversion. Conversion happens through experience and confidence. Conviction happens out of necessity and fear. Now this can take place concerning many aspects of this industry: product, corporate executive teams, and especially compensation plans.

Here are some differences between those who have conviction and those who have conversion to their product (or compensation plan):

Conversion - Those who have conversion have no fear in what they are presenting. They are comfortable with who they are, what they are presenting or sharing, and the effect it may have in someone else's life. They have this confidence because they have truly experienced it in their lives. They have used the product and lived the effects themselves. There is a sense of excitement, peace, and to some extent, love.

Conviction - Those who only have experienced conviction (for whatever reason) often times will display some uncomfortable sense of urgency in what they are expressing. They usually try too hard to share the product, and often times talk about over-the-top experiences or stories that they heard from their upline and not experiences that they themselves have had. Yet, the largest key here is that they are much more prone to argument, debate, and confrontation in the defense of their product. This may sound a little weird, but the more someone fights about something, the more fearful they are (subconsciously) that they are wrong. There is an old proverb which says, "For without was fighting, and within were fears". When someone aggressively defends, it shows lack of confidence, and they are often desperately trying to convince you so that they can secretly convince themselves.

BE AN EASY SELL

As a result of all that has been said so far - TRY the product, and use the product regularly. Be an easy sell!

If you are considering distributing the product, you need to actually play with the product. The best way to do this is to be the "easy sell". I know this might sound a little counterproductive from where we were a few paragraphs ago, but hopefully this will make sense. Don't force yourself to gain instant conviction for the product, but allow yourself to be converted by the product. This means that you do not make up your mind about the product until you use the product. But when you use the product, you use it as if you have already been entirely sold on the product. This means that you follow exactly whatever regime that is suggested.

If you are considering a 30 day weight loss program, you become an easy sell, and you buy the program. Then you follow it to the letter, as if you already know that it is going to work. In this, you also make sure that you take keen notes on everything that takes place in the process. You document how you feel the day before you start, and then document the process through the 30 days. Then, at the end, you take a very detailed evaluation of the program and determine for yourself if it worked – and if it worked, document whether you liked it. We all know tons of diet programs that work, but many of them, we have loathed every minute of. This now gives you the experience and opportunity to be converted to the product rather than convinced to gain conviction. Too many people do not even give themselves the opportunity to have the experience of true conversion to a product or service.

This works for every product and every service. If it is a juice, buy a case and try it for a month. If it is a service, enroll in the service and try it for a month. Remember the key here isn't to find a product that you like, it is to find a product that you will share. There is no shame in taking the time to invest in researching different potential products. Every retail store researches and tries numerous products before it narrows its focus to what is on the shelf, and why shouldn't you do the same.

Now, here is a small hint, and I will talk about this in the next few chapters, but often times, it will be cheaper for you to purchase these products as a Distributor. Many companies will raise the cost of the Retail price to the point that it would be cheaper for you to pay the membership or distributor fee and pay for the product at wholesale rather than buying it at retail. There is no shame in doing that, just be aware that because you have enrolled as a Distributor, that doesn't mean that you need to engage in that company or gain that conviction to sell. In these circumstances, you just need to remind yourself that you are just trying the product and being frugal at the same time. There is also no shame in buying it on the internet or through eBay either - if it is possible.

THE KNOWLEDGE FALLACY & THE FIRE HYDRANT

Now, at this junction in our discussion, I would suppose that many readers would expect the next few sections to discuss the importance of understanding your product. While there is a great deal of importance in understanding your product and what it stands for, we need to be aware that we do not need to know everything about the product. In fact, in many situations, knowing too much about the product can be detrimental to your success.

Time and time again, I see new associates who get so excited about the product that they go out and learn every little thing that they can about the product. This isn't a bad action, yet the immediate consequence of undisciplined knowledge is usually bad for business; this may also be termed as knowing too much about a product.

Usually, what results in this degree of research and knowledge is *the fire hydrant effect*. This is when contact is made with someone who shows a little interest in what you are sharing, and the knowledgeable associate suddenly becomes a freshly-tapped fire hydrant of information, spraying them (often drowning them) with an in-depth conversation of the fine intricacies of the product and how it will do everything (even possibly create world peace). After anywhere between a three to twenty minute bath in shared intelligence, the individual standing on the receiving end feels extremely overwhelmed, and either cannot believe such information or determines that it was too much to comprehend in one sitting and is no longer interested. When you are fishing and get a bite, you can yank too hard to set the hook – and tear the hook right out of the fish.

Another consequence to this is almost worse. What if you still kept that person interested in your product? They loved what they heard, and they end up loving the product. You explain to them the power of network marketing and the great company you are a part of, and they agree to enroll right then and there. Congratulations! This is seen as the best case scenario, right?

Maybe not. Because of your overwhelming spray of intellect concerning the product, you have just created a level of expectation in the new associate that you have just enrolled.

They now expect and feel that in order to do what you have just done (built your business), they, too, need to understand the product to the same degree. This new associate is now much LESS likely to share anything about the product to anyone else because of his fear of not knowing enough. To some extent, you have just done him an injustice by sharing your overabundance of knowledge.

The sad part, when I see this, is that these individuals who get so excited about the spray of knowledge they receive (and they are few and far between) also would have more than likely been just as interested with a more passive approach - focusing on the experiences that someone might have had versus the knowledge that someone has on the topic.

This is the knowledge fallacy: that knowing more is conducive to selling more – and it is false. Now, that is not to say that you shouldn't study about your favorite product if that interests you, but you need to be aware of how you share your abundance of knowledge with the world around you. Remember, people really love to discover things themselves, and if you can show them the way and allow them to learn on their own, they will have a greater sense of satisfaction with their choices and their own knowledge.

THE POWER OF CONFIDENCE

Now, out of all of the discussions above, one might read this and come under the impression that it is more important not to seek a greater knowledge of your respective product. This is not the primary intent of this section, but used only to emphasize the importance of confidence. It is far more important to carry and share your confidence concerning the product, much more so than anything else you might hear from your upline, at a meeting, or even read on the internet. You can learn all you want about a product, but you should really only share what you are confident about through your own experiences.

This confidence bred from your own experiences is not only essential to your success in whatever you choose to work with, but it is essential to your well-being as you work with your choice company. We need to feel good about what we are buying and what we are sharing in order for us not to feel like we are "selling" something, or even worse, being taken advantage of. We believe that the level of conviction we carry for something speaks about us as a person, but it is really the level of confidence we carry concerning what we are sharing that truly speaks volumes.

This confidence can sometimes be found in the researching of a product or the increase of knowledge about the technology or proprietary process. Although this type of research could yield such effects it is important to note that it is positive action for the purpose of increasing your confidence and not to increase your salesmanship directly (remember not to become the fire hydrant). More often, this confidence is gained in the experiences surrounding the product in your own life and the lives of those around you.

THE INDIRECT PRODUCT

For some, the product means less. These are people who are confident in their ability to sell candy to a dentist office, and there are some who can do it. These are natural-born salesmen and women, and they are out there. Chances are we have met many of them throughout our lives, and if you are reading this book – there is an even greater chance that you are not one of them.

Yet, with that said, as we discuss product, there is one additional product that always needs to be considered – and that is the indirect product. Indirect products are concepts that are being sold in addition to whatever someone is physically purchasing through the transaction. Notice that I used the word "sold" because if these indirect products are part of the equation, they are being sold, not shared. The most traditional indirect product is the compensation plan (which will be discussed further in the following chapters). Compensation plans can be products as well, and can be utilized to try and sell additional indirect products or concepts such as financial freedom, trips, incentives, and "living the dream".

There are additional indirect products in network marketing that are a little more indiscriminant such as: a corporate executive team and the experience they carry, the interpersonal relationships of an organization (parties, meetings, etc), and even the market place. We already discussed in an earlier chapter how the major product being sold in this industry is the industry itself and the power that is in network marketing – this by definition is an indirect product.

These additional indirect products are mentioned for two reasons:

First, knowing that these are additional products that are being presented, it is often important to be able to recognize when they are being presented to you as a product. As you learn more about the product, you need to analyze how much of each of these indirect products you are being "sold" on. You need to identify if they are emphasizing one aspect over another in a presentation or in the corporate philosophy, and why they may be neglecting another one of these aspects. Doing this type of analysis, can help you see where potential weaknesses within a company may be. If you notice that they never mention the executive team, maybe it is because they are not comfortable with their experience and do not want to highlight them. If there is no mention of the compensation plan, the question lingers as to whether or not it will be a competitive plan. In addition, you may need to remind yourself that these are indirect products, and often times there are circumstances where that is all that you will hear: corporate experience, compensation plan, industry timing, and the power of networking. When you evaluate all of these things, you may find them true and faithful, but ask yourself, "Why are the indirect products highlighted instead of the primary product?" That is always a great question to ask.

Second, the industry can be extremely competitive, and there are numerous products that are of stellar quality; to discover a life-changing, category-creating product sometimes is no longer enough. Knowing these indirect products can also give you greater confidence in the presentation of your product. Although you may or may not focus on these indirect products, knowing them, and being able to answer questions about them confidently, can give you a remarkable competitive edge in the industry. Some of the largest leaders in the industry learned this very early on in their careers, and would always ask these hard questions, which lead the companies being asked to recognize how important these indirect products could be. The disappointing part is that many newer companies took the importance of these indirect products and misinterpreted their positioning in the hierarchy of industry needs. Now, there are many companies who are hoping that these indirect products will give them success in lue of a powerful primary product.

THE BEST ADVICE FOR YOUR BEST PRODUCT

The most important advice that is given in circumstances where someone is considering a company is to make sure you pick a product that you can get behind and that you are going to use. Not only use, but that you will be willing to purchase on a regular basis.

I always tell people, "Pick a product that you want, and that you wouldn't mind purchasing or using regularly, even if you were not going to make any money with it". You need to make sure you are not going to get tired of product before you start bringing in the money. I am convinced that many people give up on their business, not because they can't do it, but because they picked the wrong product, have a whole load of it in their garage (because they are not using it), and they can't bring themselves to purchase another box of it. Don't do that! Join a company with product that you feel you can afford and that you will consume or use on a regular basis, preferably a product that you would purchase even if it wasn't a network marketing opportunity, and even if you never made a dime from it.

I was once given some great advice: Never buy anything in the heat of the moment if you have to buy it right now to get the deal. That is usually the sign of a bad deal the next morning. That advice has kept me out of a lot of financial trouble and deals. Let's borrow from that concept, and let me give you another application: Don't buy product just because it is a network marketing opportunity. If it is not a product that you would buy or use otherwise, than why would anyone else?

If you are excited about the opportunity, but not about the product – take some time and reconsider your choice. More likely than not, you will be able to find an excitement for both from another company. There are options in the world of network marketing.

COPY CATS: NO FEAR

As a unique product is more successful than the retail market expected, there will always be copy cats in the stores.

These copy cats will take the primary concept and try to make it cheap and market it as easier to purchase. This is going to happen; expect it. Do not over react when this takes place. If anything, this brings validation to the work that you are doing with your product. Now, others are going to hear about it, and more likely than not, your company will ensure that you are filled to the brim with information detailing why your product is still superior.

This has happened over and over in the industry, and will happen again and again. This is not preventable – but the great part about a great company and product that is being duplicated in another market is that what made your business successful is never ONLY the product, but is the amalgamation of the product and all other indirect products your company offers. This is why we cover more than just product in this text. Keep calm; any overreaction in this environment can breed fear in your team.

Just remember, no matter what your product is – you sell more than a product. You sell opportunity, freedom, well-being, and a chance to do something new.

Thoughts to take away from this chapter:
- Gain Comfort, Conversion, and Confidence about the product
- Be aware of Indirect Products and how they are used and can be used to build your business
- Be an easy sell and try the product or service
- Find a product that you can use and enjoy sharing
- Do not fear the Copy Cat

CHAPTER 5

THE PRODUCT:
TYPE, POSITIONING, AND LIFESPAN

Regardless of the level of knowledge you gain on any particular product, or your level of salesmanship, everyone would benefit from knowing where each of their potential products are positioned in the industry. Understanding the positioning of the product in the industry also helps to regulate expectations. As you know what your product is, not only to you, but to the industry, you are able to understand the appeal that others might have towards it. By knowing what type of product you are dealing with in the market, you can have a greater outlook on where your business is going and where it will be in the next few years. By being able to identify the different types of products in the industry, you can create a realistic business plan and maximize your time by identifying what product type is best for you.

My first introduction to the network marketing industry was because there was a product that I fell in love with and believed in, and the only way I could obtain the product was to become a distributor for that company.

Throughout my time in the industry, I have learned that there are too many products to count that are distributed through network marketing. If you want to buy it, or have ever bought something, you could probably find an avenue for it in the industry. Yet, with as many companies and products as are out there, there are really only five types or categories of products that are directly related to the development of the company, growth patterns, and overall lifespan of a company in the industry. These product types are:

- The exclusive/unique product
- The standard product
- The enhanced product
- The marketed product
- The opportunity product

Some types of products are more likely to grow fast, some more steady, and some are more volatile. Some demand more organic growth through product training and education, and some require sheer excitement and ignorance in order to grow. The reality is that success (however you have defined it) can be found within each of these product types. The trick is identifying and being aware of the product type that you are working with, and creating your expectations around the realities that surround your product. Therefore, the intention here is to discuss the definition, appeal, drawbacks, lifespan, and building strategies of all five of the product types.

When talking about these topics, please note that we are discussing the product's contribution to each of these product types and their associated topic. There are more contributing factors to a company's appeal, drawbacks, lifespan, and building strategies than just the product; and many of the additional contributing factors will be discussed in more detail in the following chapters.

Please keep in mind that the examples of each of these products are extremes and are rarely seen in as pure a form as they are presented here. Really, you will find that many products can cover a number of different product types, and therefore can inherit numerous appeals, difficulties, and lifespan issues.

THE EXCLUSIVE/UNIQUE PRODUCT: THE DEFINITION

In my introduction to the industry, the products that I fell in love with and felt like I couldn't live without were exclusive products. These were products that were extremely unique to the retail market, and they couldn't be found easily without going through this network marketing company. They had something specific and unique that I wanted that I couldn't find anywhere else.

The exclusive product usually means that the company has an edge or corners a market for the product or the product category. These are the real "category-creating" products. This can also mean that they are on the cutting edge of some research or propriety process that allows them to create this unique opportunity. Often times, the product is so unique that network marketing is the only way to legitimately sell the product, as it would take far too much marketing to bring it into a mainstream market and make it profitable.

Of course, as these unique products increase in popularity, there will always be copycats or cheaper retail versions once there is marketable success with the product. So it is still important to have a good enhanced story, not only about why your company's products are fantastic, but why they will never be beat in quality.

Now, when I talk about an exclusive product being a unique concept, it is important to understand that all network marketing products have some degree of uniqueness; there is always something that tries to set it apart from the rest, and that is what we call marketing. Just because there is something unique about the product doesn't make it an exclusive product.

What makes it an exclusive product isn't a specific ingredient, or a unique process, but a unique concept. Something that the mainstream retail market will not touch with a ten foot pole until a network marketing company creates enough of a demand. What makes the exclusive product "exclusive" is the concept.

THE EXCLUSIVE/UNIQUE PRODUCT: THE APPEAL

The exclusive products are the easiest products to get behind, because they are the easiest to be converted to and have great conviction for. They have the greatest potential to excite someone, or create a spark in someone's understanding as to why they need the product. Exclusive products make us feel exclusive, like we have something that the rest of the world doesn't.

This type of product carries with it a degree of necessary conversion to it. Often times, these products are a little off base at the time that they are developed and released – and it takes years for the concept to spread into the mainstream. These products take a degree of training to understand and see their grand purpose.

In exclusive product companies, the appeal to the company is usually only seen through the appeal for the product. The draw to the company is not the compensation plan, the executive team, or the possibilities of network marketing – it is getting their hands on that product. Yet, in a business stand point, these exclusive products also appeal to the one-on-one direct marketer, because these products yield a greater retention, and the product conversion creates a greater sense of uniqueness and exclusivity within the new associate. It can sometimes be easier to retain after someone has been enrolled.

THE EXCLUSIVE/UNIQUE PRODUCT: THE DRAWBACK

Exclusive products now are few and far between. Everyone tries to be seen as exclusive, because that is marketable, but few really are in today's market.

The major drawback is that real exclusive products do not appeal to the mainstream. The very thing that defines them as exclusive, their uniqueness, actually hinders their growth and the growth of their distributors.

In these companies, there is a great deal of emphasis on product training. The more training the new distributor gets, the greater the conversion to the product, and the more stability the company has. The problem with this is that education takes time and slows duplication. I have rarely seen a successful exclusive product really merge the gap between product education and business education, although many have tried.

By the shear nature of the conversion of the individual to the product, the desire to learn more is instilled. When that desire in kindled, it is hard to replace the desire to learn with the desire to share, or even the confidence that they can share without having as much knowledge of the product as possible.

In conclusion, the major drawback is slow growth with a great degree of desired education and training on the product. This is usually termed "organic growth", meaning that person-to-person contact is almost necessary to excite someone about the product (and not the company).

THE EXCLUSIVE/UNIQUE PRODUCT: THE LIFESPAN

The lifespan of exclusive products are the reason why everyone tries to look like an exclusive product company. Most real exclusive product companies are long lasting and steady growers. These companies, although they grow slowly (relatively speaking), they grow with high stability. The education that is perceived by the distributor to be required actually creates an extremely loyal distributor force and bolsters retention.

These companies may take ten to fifteen years to move out of coach and reach business class in the airplane, but when they get there they are there to stay.

THE EXCLUSIVE/UNIQUE PRODUCT: BUILDING STRATEGY

The major difficulty is the need to educate. As stated above, many have tried to merge the desire for the business and the desire for the product.

One strategy that I have seen work in these companies is to only focus on the product during presentations. Once people know that they need and want the product, there is usually a very small pitch concerning the benefits of becoming a wholesale distributor, which would allow them to purchase the already expensive product at a discount. This usually is as far as the opportunity pitch goes for the time being. When the new distributor or associate enrolls in these companies, it is not to start a business, but to save money by not purchasing at retail price. After the new distributor enrolls, there is usually additional training on the product, where the goal is to excite them to share the product, and educate them enough to give them the confidence to do so.

THE STANDARD PRODUCT: THE DEFINITION

These are usually products or services that are not at all unique to the retail market, but also include many different types of products. Sometimes, the general idea is to create a catalogue company which may offer numerous types of everyday products (possibly with some high quality pitch behind them) and then try and sell you on the opportunity by saying, "if you are going to be buying these products anyways, you might as well buy them here and have the potential of earning some income in the process". This is usually the case with companies that may try to offer cleaning supplies, phone and cable service, or even toilet paper.

THE STANDARD PRODUCT: THE APPEAL

These are nice if the product or service is something that you are really going to use and buy regardless, as long as they are reasonably priced. My philosophy is, if the same amount of money is going to be spent buying toilet paper, then why not buy it through a network marketing channel. This way, you get the product, you will usually get a higher quality product, and you have the opportunity to make some additional income as you have others do the same thing.

These products are also relatively easy to teach and train upon, because they are products that are used every day. Here, the greater job you do is selling the indirect products (network marketing, compensation plan, industry timing), that the company offers the greater success and excitement one would have. These products also usually carry with it a perception of higher quality. Also, gold-laced toilet paper tends to make you look really high class, and can also appeal to those who want you to know it.

THE STANDARD PRODUCT: THE DRAWBACK

The major drawback of standard products or services is that you need to be really good at utilizing those additional indirect products in order to grow your business. In these circumstances you are not really selling a product, you are selling an opportunity – and usually the experienced network marketers are the greatest at playing this game. The standard product sell isn't for everyone.

Because of the lack of uniqueness, it can sometimes be increasingly difficult to teach someone the importance of buying something from you that they can just buy from the store (and on sale). This becomes especially true if the pricing is not competitive or reasonable to the retail market that they will see at the store. These companies also suffer quite a bit during recessions. Although the industry usually does well through recessions, this is because people are looking to make more money and not because they are looking to pay more for products they can get on sale somewhere else. Recessions are great for unique products and opportunity products – but are disastrous for standard products.

THE STANDARD PRODUCT: THE LIFESPAN

If a standard-product company can really get past the launch, and are successful at making it through a few global economic bumps, then they can really be around for the long haul. Companies that sell standard products can last longer than many other company types, but there are fewer that actually make it that long. Most of the successful standard-product companies that have survived have done miracles making a name and a culture for themselves over time. This is true, so much so, that usually if you were invited to join, you were usually invited to party to do so, and were probably being sold just as much on the culture as anything else. If the culture is already developed in the company, then it speaks to their stability; if the culture is hard to find, then their lifespan will be shortened.

THE STANDARD PRODUCT: THE BUILDING STRATEGY

Usually, the building strategy for the standard product is trying to display the culture. Utilizing parties and direct one-on-one contact is usually the best way to get people involved in the product. In building a standard-product business, you also need to be comfortably versed in the indirect products that the company offers, and allow that confidence to show. By creating a network of friends, and allowing everyone to gather regularly to share experiences or life stories, always centering the product or company in the middle of such activities, you will be able to build a business slowly but steadily, and increase the well-being of those around you with the culture you create at your party – which ultimately can become an indirect product of your organization as well.

THE ENHANCED PRODUCT: THE DEFINITION

When a standard product is too expensive, it almost always naturally becomes an enhanced product, not necessarily out of truth, but out of necessity. These are products that take a standard product or concept, something that anyone can easily access through a different model, and enhances it in order to create a greater appeal to it. The company will find some new research or technology, and add something remarkable to it, or take away something negative from it. Yet, these enhancements always come with a cost, and these products are often times much more expensive than buying similar "unenhanced" products in the grocery store. These enhanced claims are often necessary in order to justify the additional cost for the product. Classic examples of these types of products are nutritional vitamin supplements; you can buy a similar product at the grocery story, but if you buy it through the network marketing channel, you not only will pay much more, but you will gain a significant amount of additional benefit from the product (as a result of better sourcing, proprietary process, or some technological advancement).

THE ENHANCED PRODUCT: THE APPEAL

These products are enhanced and therefore, are often better than what is being sold elsewhere. When these products are actually better than other similar products, and it is relatively easier to prove, it can be much easier to share and to allow others to experience. When a product is enhanced, you not only increase the marketability of a product, you also are using a general concept from another, more known product concept. Usually, these enhanced products are based from products that everyone already knows how to use, and they have already used something similar in the past. Supplements are always the best example of this. Everyone has used supplements, and to some extent, almost everyone agrees that some supplementation is already necessary. With enhanced products, half of the job of sharing the product is already done, they already will understand the basic concept and need for your product. It is now only the enhancement that needs to be justified. These are definitely products that need to be experienced in order to justify the enhancement of the standard product.

Also, traditionally these companies may have a more balanced approach of building their organizations. This is usually a decent mix of both product-based training, as well as opportunity-based trainings. So, although these companies will not explode out of the gate, they will grow a little faster than unique products, and will attract a good mix of product users and building leaders to create steady growth. This is often a result of not needing extensive product training in order to use, experience, or share.

THE ENHANCED PRODUCT: THE DRAWBACK

The most difficult part of using an enhanced product is trying to justify the additional cost it takes to purchase the product. Often times, the reasons why one would be able to justify such a purchase can come off hokey and a little over the top. These enhanced products can also yield a slower growing organization.

Enhanced products also yield a larger market of competition quicker. The larger and sooner the organization is successful in marketing the enhanced product successfully, the sooner a product developer with greater resources develops a similar product with a lower mark-up. These products are easier to duplicate in the retail market because they are literally already developed with only a few adjustments. Often times, you may find yourself competing with possibly even higher quality in the retail market place. This competition, if you have built your business on product users, can demolish an organization if the retail market is able to significantly beat the current pricing. The only time that network marketing companies and organizations are not negatively affected by this level of competition is if it becomes large enough to keep the leaders working and building because of their earning power.

THE ENHANCED PRODUCT: THE LIFESPAN

These can sometimes be the trickiest of all companies, because sometimes it just isn't different enough, and sometimes it can be too different to succeed. The only real way to judge the lifespan of these companies is by its leadership in the organization, its leadership in the corporate office, and the other indirect products. Even at that, the best way to see if it will be a successful enhanced-product company is to see what happens with them. Starting with one is risky, but usually if you are able to engage when it is already successful, you can be sure it will be a longer haul than others. These are 99% of the companies out there that are starting today, and these are also 99.9% of companies that fail. If it is a starting enhanced-product company, consider waiting around to ensure they will be around.

THE ENHANCED PRODUCT: THE BUILDING STRATEGY

Consider this an open bar, and use whatever works. These are a little easier to balance a business around, because they are able to sell to the product user and increase the efficacy of the product, while not needing a significant amount of product training time. This is more of an experience product, where a customer may take the product and experience the change or difference between similar products, and no training is necessary or is at least minimized. Let people experience the product, but get them excited about any other indirect products your company may offer.

THE MARKETED PRODUCT: THE DEFINITION

These products or services are frauds. These are products that are not enhanced, they are not exclusive (or if they are they shouldn't be because of their real value), these products are overpriced, and they have claims that are unsubstantiated, false, and not even possible. Sadly, these exist, and are disappointing when they come around. This is when CEOs see success in the industry and want to start a company, not knowing anything about product development or marketing – and the importance of having a good combination of both. Marketed products are always an illusion of claims and sometimes are not real products, or offers no unique service. The success of these companies is based entirely around the success of selling indirect products (often times equally fraudulently).

THE MARKETED PRODUCT: THE APPEAL

The appeal of a marketed product is the degree upon which they can make the indirect products appealing. This is often the "sell" of the compensation plan (which is usually designed to over pay in order to create growth), the industry timing, or the ease of their recruiting program (lead generators) that will do all of the work for you. At the end of the day, there is no primary product that anyone cares about. The appeal to some leaders is if they can identify the imagined value of the indirect products, they are confident that they can get in and make as much money as possible, and then jump ship before it sinks.

THE MARKETED PRODUCT: THE DRAWBACK

The drawback here is hopefully obvious. These are not real companies, and although they may seem legitimate in the short run – no amount of success will make them legitimate in the long run. Many of these companies are funded by people who are aware of this, and would like to make as much money as possible in a short period of time. When the boat starts to sink, they are also prepared for it, and realize that it is more profitable to let the boat sink and start another one than try to save it. Watch out for these.

THE MARKETED PRODUCT: THE LIFESPAN

The lifespan of the marketed product is varied and is directly determined by how successful they are and how quickly that success takes place. The key here, though, is to realize that it is limited, regardless. There will always be a time when these products end, or at least the opportunity surrounding them will no longer be available or as profitable as they once were. It could be six months, a year, or two years – but the longer it goes, the more damaging it will be when it falls.

THE MARKETED PRODUCT: THE BUILDING STRATEGY

If you are going to risk the endeavor to enter into a marketed product, the most important thing that you will need to know in building is that it is a marketed product. Know and be aware that you have limited time with this product or opportunity. You can make money here, but know that it will not last. Understand that you need to move, and you need to move fast, and at the end of the day, you need to be prepared to jump ship – and start to try to recover any relationships that may be hurt in the process. I am aware of a number of close associates who have been very successful (financially) from these types of opportunities, but it has all been based on the knowledge that they were preparing from day one to jump ship when it started to sink. Knowing that it is coming won't prevent it from happening, it just doesn't make it a surprise when it happens, and it can often help you maximize your earnings in the mean time. This is usually for the hard core network marketers without souls.

Warning: Even if you are a professional network marketer and you feel that you can accomplish something in the "Churn and Burn", I would highly recommend do it under a pseudo-name or business entity. The reason for this is that even the greatest leaders in the industry have names to uphold, and if someone is associated with too many "Churn and Burn" companies, then they will be seen as the marker for the "Churn and Burn". People will stop following you, first because few people have it in them to do it a second or third time, and second because they will stop having confidence in your abilities to make a company work – because they won't have the same or a similar philosophy as you. Even doing this sometimes makes it impossible for your name not to be affiliated with it.

THE OPPORTUNITY PRODUCT: THE DEFINITION

Opportunity Products are usually products that are solely developed with the intent of creating a network marketing company around it. These are usually designed specifically with the marketing around the product. Often times, these are products that have some degree of quality to them, but are not usually intended to be of the highest quality. These are usually created to be a good mix between the marketing of the product and profitability – so they develop them with the cost of goods and production in mind. These have been designed from the product ingredients, to the shape and style of the packaging, to the compensation plan, all to appear superior and marketable – not for product efficacy.

These are the real mover products. These are the products that are sold as if they are exclusive, enhanced, and must be in every household – but are really created solely for the purpose of creating an opportunity. These also could be considered fraud or marketed products to many people because the product may, or may not, do anything, and conceivably was created for the sole purpose of creating a network marketing company. The difference between these products and marketed or fraud products is that they are much more successful, because they were created or constructed by people who knew what they were doing. The company knew that in order to have a good opportunity product, they also needed to appeal to the next door neighbor and product user with the product – so it needed to have a story of uniqueness. They knew enough to know that they needed really great marketing to appeal to the business man who may never really ever take the product, but wanted to make money. They knew that they needed to try to fill every marketing role possible. This type of product is usually the hardest to spot for some and the easiest to spot for others. One trick I find in spotting these products is when they are "one-product wonders". This is when the whole company is based and only offers this one product, because all you will need is that one product or ingredient.

THE OPPORTUNITY PRODUCT: APPEAL

The appeal to these products is that they are usually able to create a massive amount of duplication, because they have a great deal of support in marketing around it. These opportunity products are usually backed by a competitive compensation plan and a number of well-paid leaders to help most individuals in the organization gain a potential for success.

As these products are built and fashioned around the opportunity of network marketing, they are created with the image and profitability of the distributor in mind. These are good products to try and build a business with because they will have a nicely crafted story behind it, and it will fit nicely into the compensation plan the company tried to launch with.

Duplication is also something that is usually fashioned in the creation of the product, and at times, can be seen as easier to build with. As stated previously, these usually are single-product companies. These single-product opportunity companies make it easier to create and sustain duplication, as the only training that everyone needs on the product is that it is good for you, or will help you in some way.

THE OPPORTUNITY PRODUCT: DRAWBACK

Although these types of products have built substantial organizations and companies, it is difficult to sustain long-term growth after five or six years. This is because people get bored, and they start looking for new things. By the fifth year of a company (if it has had any degree of success), it will also have a number of copy cats who may be able to provide a greater value. This forces these opportunity product companies into trying to create a "product line" and merging from an opportunity company into something more of a product-based company – hoping to get that level of stability. The problem with this action is that the inevitable introductions of other products flies in the face of the marketing that has made the product successful, and therefore, this wonder product is no longer all you need – and the company contradicts its own culture. This is a long-term problem, and very few opportunity-based product companies have ever successfully shifted their clientele into believing the product-based culture.

If they are also only a one-product company, they run into the problem of introducing new products that are similar enough to the standard philosophy, and still keep people engaged and interested in the development of the company. An internal problem that takes place when they are successful in the new product launch, because it is close to the philosophy, is that they find themselves competing with their own resources. If the new product replaces the purchase of the original product, then all they have done is shifted the purchase of product from the old product to the new product, increasing their business by zero, while increasing the cost of administration. In these opportunity companies, this type of growth is necessary, although not necessarily financially smart. If the company is not well enough positioned or funded, this type of questionable growth can really place the company at risk over time. These actions ultimately only postpone the inevitable.

THE OPPORTUNITY: LIFESPAN

When these companies are successful, they usually last between three to six years. These companies are usually the fastest growing and most successful companies for a time – and then after they peak, fall relatively quickly. The trick with building your business, considering this lifespan, is to be committed for a time in order to generate the wealth you desire, and then when your organization starts to plateau, you keep an eye out for something more out there. Generating a good amount of income for three to five years in a company can be rather amazing. It is also good to keep in mind that just because it starts to slow down or fall after three to five years, that doesn't mean that it will drop immediately – any residual income can still show up in your bank account for years to come in the future. All this means is that the standard expected growth of the company is no longer as steady as it was in the past.

THE OPPORTUNITY: BUILDING STRATEGY

These can be much easier to build if you are willing to put in the work and be committed. They usually do have a compensation plan and strategy that are worked out and the leadership in the field to support it. Because they are usually "one-hit-wonder" products, they are also easier to teach and train people in the product – because there is less to train on. It also becomes much easier to talk about and to get others talking about it. The story is usually well enough crafted and marketed that it helps to sell the product rather successfully. When building these companies, you need to be committed, and pretend that it will last forever. By doing this, you will be able to share or sell (whichever you choose) your product with conviction and with a higher level of conversion.

These products usually carry with them a high amount of indirect products. Focus on the indirect products with the product, or even in lue of the product. Make these indirect products (company, culture, compensation plan) and their greatness synonymous with the product.

THE HYPOTHETICAL BEST PRODUCT

It is important to understand that there is no such thing as the "best" product. The term "best" can only relatively be defined. Each person is looking for something different when they are looking for a product, and so it is important to understand that there is no such thing as a universal product. There are some products that are easier to use, some that are easier to sell, and some that are more effective than others – but none of these characteristics really can denote the "best" of everything for everyone. Some want to make money with their product, some only care about the indirect products, and some want to be healed with their product and have conviction for something.

The best product is the product that you are looking for: a product that you can buy, that you can sell, that you can share, that you can feel good about, that you can make money with, or that you can even manipulate in order find success with (if that is your ultimate goal). My intention with detailing the different type of products wasn't to tell you that one was better than the other, but that you could be prepared and understand what to expect with either. Money, success, and well-being could be found with any product – as long as it is respected as what it is, and your actions are in association with what should be expected throughout its lifespan.

Thoughts to take away from this chapter:
- Understanding your product type can help you plan effectively (short term and long-term)
- Know your products appeal, drawbacks, lifespan, and building strategy.
- There is no perfect product, just a great product and culture for you.

CHAPTER 6

COMPENSATION PLANS: THE BASICS AND GENERAL RULES

Despite common conversation in the industry, there is no perfect or best compensation plan. The value of any compensation plan is all relative to what the company and what the distributor is trying to accomplish. Each company has different goals and desires, a specific culture which will require a different type of behavior incentivized by the compensation plan. Each distributor has a different building technique, and despite the ultimate goal of making money, needs the plan to have a particular structure in order to succeed. Remember, everyone is different, and everyone has different hopes, dreams, and aspirations; and therefore, not everyone can excel in every plan.

In the most basic concepts, a compensation plan is designed to do two things: compensate financially for sales that have been made and to incentivize or promote a particular behavior within an organization that will result in more sales. Most distributors focus primarily on the first one, and how they can make money. Most corporate environments *should* focus on how to incentivize behavior. In this relationship, the power of a good compensation plan finds the medium in being able to satisfy both sides of this equation.

With all of that said, it is sometimes harder to see the reality that no plan concept is inherently better than any other plan. Yet, there is a distinct difference between a competitive plan and an uncompetitive plan – and competitiveness is entirely separate from the general plan concept or structure. Two nearly identical compensation plans, from two different companies, both selling the same product type, can both look competitive, but when you look at the nitty-gritty – one will be competitive and one will not be. It is often the small things that make the difference within the plan and how it is managed. That is the intent of this chapter and the next chapter – to help you identify those seemingly small concepts surrounding the plan that can be monstrous in indentifying the competitive plans over the hollow plans.

So far in this text, we have spent a chapter reviewing the industry, your own abilities, and your sponsor's abilities. We have also spent two chapters on products, detailing some general concepts, as well as the potential appeals and benefits of each product type to help you match the product to your personality and goals. We will now take the next two chapters and deal with the compensation plan; first, focusing on some basic and general rules that apply to every plan throughout the industry, independent of type, category or product; second, we will focus on the type of plan and the personality of each (as we did similar to the product).

MARKETED VS. REALITY

Throughout the next few chapters it is critical for you to remember this one concept: there is a distinct difference between how the plan is marketed and the reality of the plan. For instance, if the plan is marketed to be high-paying and easy, it looks really good, but if the small things are in the right place, the reality still could be that is it is hard and low-paying, with a lot of breakage to the company (to be discussed later). Just because a plan says it pays out a lot doesn't mean it actually does. So, as you read through the following concepts, take time to really consider the answers, and as always, try to ask the right questions. If the compensation plan literature says one thing, really ask yourself if that is true, and ask if there is a possibility that it could be wrong. The great part about compensation plan literature is there is usually something within the literature itself that inadvertently gives its own limitations away. Review all the compensation plan literature available, and after reading this book, keep your eyes peeled for some red flags.

Compensation plan literature is a tricky topic as it relates to this subject, because the design of most of this type of literature is marketing and not for educational purposes. It is designed to look good and sell the compensation plan as an indirect product. Therefore, the terminology used is usually not the clearest, and things can be said that are only half true "in the name of marketing". This just widens the gap between the marketed appearance of a plan and the reality of the plan.

LITERATURE

A good sign of good compensation plan literature is more than just a single-page brochure. I personally find it humorous when companies only offer a small single-page document on their plan – it is obviously just for marketing and not for education. There is always more than a single page of compensation plan information in any plan! This doesn't do anyone justice, as the new distributor still really doesn't know how to make money, and therefore, is not able to engage as much as they could if they had developed the appropriate understanding of the program. This ultimately leaves the company with less at the end of the day as a result of "in the name of marketing".

There can always be a single-page brochure, and frankly there should be for those who just want to understand the general concepts. Yet, in these circumstances, there should also be more advanced literature that should give pages of information. Often times, these will be seen in the form of little booklets, and are kind of the mix between marketing and education. This is usually a good sign.

As companies develop, they should also eventually offer on their back office, or in the official Policies and Procedures, a more detailed, almost technical document on the compensation plan. It usually is not critical that everyone read these types of documents, but sometimes they can yield a slightly competitive edge. They also help to eliminate any questions on how things are actually calculated. These types of technical documents are more designed by the legal team and the compensation plan department to protect the company against any fraudulent payout claims or calculations.

Don't be too concerned if the company you are looking into doesn't have this document (as long as they are only a few years old), because it takes time to see what is actually happening in the field, and the commission engine to document it properly, real talent to interpret the data, and remarkable skill in understanding this data to write these documents so that they are clear and are more of an asset to the company than a liability. Sadly, not enough companies have this level of skill under their belt or on their staff, and therefore, "don't see the need for this type of document". These documents are a really good sign of an open and mature company.

Therefore, it should go without saying that the first step in evaluating a compensation plan is to understand the plan. The first step in understanding the plan is reading the available literature, and then asking the right questions.

If you are really concerned about the compensation plan, read all the literature available and strive to understand it – that will yield a knowledge that less than 5% of the industry has obtained about their own plans. Yet, keep in mind that just like products, the "Knowledge Fallacy" applies to compensation plans as well.

THE KNOWLEDGE FALLACY AND COMPENSATION PLANS

The Knowledge Fallacy, as it applies to compensation plans is: The more you know about the compensation plan means the more you make from the compensation plan. This is FALSE!

It was early in my consulting career, and I was meeting with some of the most successful marketers in the industry. These were individuals who would ask me to review the compensation plan from the company that they had already made a significant income with. After reviewing all of the literature on the plan, and feeling pretty confident in my knowledge, I would return to my client. Almost every client I had, that asked me to do this task, then brought me to a display of their organization, and asked me to teach them how to maximize their plan with their current company. At the end of the day, my job was to teach these extremely successful network marketers the compensation plan that they already had earned more money from than I could imagine. I was amazed! And priding myself on my experience and knowledge on compensation plans, I was a little offended the first few times it happened. It was about the fifth experience that I had, which was an exact duplication of the previous four, when I could tell I was on the cusp of learning something significant.

A few years later I found myself managing a compensation plan for a company in a corporate environment. Part of my responsibility was managing the education of the plan, as well as many other things related to the compensation plan. In this environment, I met some remarkable people and people who loved compensation plans as much as I did. These associates would come to all of my trainings, and by the end of a short while, I could quiz them on every little bit of literature and structures imaginable.

I was proud of them, and proud of the job I did for them. I had educated them on a topic that most people glaze over, and do not take the time or the consideration to learn. One day, being as proud as ever, I related in one of my trainings, the experience of my early consulting and how none of these big leaders knew half as much as they did. As I did that, they all got pretty excited, and it really increased their confidence. At the end of the meeting, I had one associate come up to me and ask very quietly, "Ryan, everyone here knows the plan, but what did those leaders know that we don't?" I looked around and realized rather quickly that I was in a room full of people who knew the compensation plan, but still did not know how to make money. No one in that room had made more than a few hundred dollars. This was a humbling experience.

Knowing the compensation plan doesn't mean you make money – working the compensation plan means you make money. The reason that those leaders made money was because they WORKED HARD at finding, recruiting, teaching, sharing, and bringing more people into their organization. That gave them more money than knowing the compensation plan.

Since then, I have changed my trainings. I always talk about how knowing the plan can help you maximize your earnings, but working on finding and bringing more people to your team will give you the earnings to maximize.

Every time I have worked on a compensation plan, I always know more than almost anyone in the world about how that plan works. I know how it is programmed. I know how people behave to it. I know how the company responds. I know the best way to build it, and all the "loop-holes". But at the end of the day, when I was cutting those checks – who was making the most money from the plan? The person who knew the most about the plan (me)? Or the person who was working the hardest at building the plan (the working associate)? I can show you my bank statements to prove it was always the associate who was building their team.

It is good to know the compensation plan and feel confident with it. Like products, knowing more about the plan increases your confidence, and therefore, increases your confidence when you talk about it. Your increased confidence can also increase your influence on others and helping them to feel confident about the plan. But please do not confuse knowledge on the compensation plan to directly affect how much money you are making in your commissions check. How hard you work will affect how much you make in your commission check.

The Basics

The compensation plan you choose to work with is critical to your success. It will affect how you build, how you sell or share, and how you earn money. The following concepts throughout the rest of this chapter are simple, but critical concepts to consider when looking at any plan, and often times are the fine print that can make or break the reality of any plan. As stated previously in the introduction to this chapter, you can have two plans that may follow all the same format and appeal to you in each area (that will be discussed in future chapters), but that may have some small adjustment made in the programming, marketing, or in how it is designed internally, that can make the difference between having something lucrative or something annoyingly impossible.

Unfortunately for the masses, many of these types of decisions are made in the corporate environments, sometimes with the distributors in mind, and sometimes with the executive team bonuses in mind; and unless you are on the inside (really on the inside), you will never be able to know. Because of this fact it is impossible for you to know everything that takes place in the corporate environment, or that may affect your commission check. This partially is why, in the coming chapters, the importance of trusting and understanding your Corporate Team will be discussed.

Fortunately, you have someone that has been on the inside of these conversations, and you have this book to help you identify the most pressing issues. The rest of this chapter is designed to help you address the most universal and common concepts that define the competitiveness of a plan - not just how competitive they *say* it is, but how competitive and lucrative it *really* is. These are ideas and principles that can help you ask the questions that apply to every type of plan.

UNDERSTANDING THE FINANCE OF COMPENSATION PLANS

The entire premise of a commission or compensation plan is to reward or compensate you financially for sales that you generate or are connected to (usually through a genealogy tree). This means that generally speaking, some product is sold for a price, and a part of that price is then given to you as a commission. This means that there has to be the sale of a product and a transaction in order for you to earn commissions.

There may be times when researching that you may find a company who will reward you for not selling a product or not creating some type of transaction. Avoid these as much as poss-ible. There is a possibility that it may be nothing more than a Marketed Product type, but it also may be a scheme to get your money, or even worse, it could be promoting illegal activity.

The most important thing to note in the transaction that takes place is that the transaction is for a specific amount. That amount now dictates the amount of money available to the com-pany, and therefore, the amount of money the company can consider paying back out to the field in the form of commis-sions. That transaction amount now needs to cover the cost of producing the product, warehousing the product, marketing the product, administering the product or company, potential expan-sion costs, and still pay a competitive amount to the distributors or sales associates in the form of commissions. The end result is that there is only so much money that can go around from the sale of a single product.

With this conclusion, the corporate team needs to be con-stantly aware of this balance between paying distributors a commission and keeping the company stable. If a product's cost of production is high, then they are limited to the amount of money left in this transaction to pay in commissions. If the com-pensation plan is too rich and pays too much, then the company is limited in their ability to pay their bills and stay in business. Ultimately, the company needs to grow and expand or the dis-tributor doesn't make anything in the end, and it needs to close its doors. When compensation plans are balanced, both sides are happy; corporate environment can thrive, and the distributor field can earn significant income.

The primary lesson here is that even though everybody wants more money, there is only so much money that can go around. It is finding a balance, and as distributors or associates, accepting that balance. The trick here is identifying if the balance exists, if the company is taking too much or if the compensation plan is paying too much – both are disastrous and sadly quite common in the industry.

BECOMING COMFORTABLE AND UNDERSTANDING EARNING LIMITATIONS

In many compensation plans, you will notice that sometimes there are benchmarks or total earning potentials on one or more of the bonuses that are offered. These are usually in more aggressive plans that allow for building the organization to be quick and profitable. These limitations can sometimes be frustrating to people, and many people expect someone like me to recommend that they look out for these limitations and avoid them. They are often surprised when I tell them to do the opposite and be weary of plans that do not have limitations. These limitations, caps, or perceived barriers actually create a strong degree of stability.

Sometimes the very limitations that are preventing you from making more money are the same limitations that made it possible for you to make what you already have made. For example, these caps may limit the amount that you earn, but because they also limited someone else from make more money, that action freed up the funds to allow you to earn the first portion of your earnings. Without those caps, the first person to qualify might have earned twice as much as he did, but left nothing for anyone that follows to earn.

Now, I am not saying that you should always accept caps and limitations as a blessing. I am saying that you should be aware that there are always things about every plan that people may feel frustrated with, but often times these frustrations are necessary for the good parts of the plan to function.

DESIGNED FOR THE MAJORITY

Compensation plans need to be designed to allow everyone to have the potential to earn a profit while building your organization in a safe and familiar way to you. The same is also true for every individual that joins that company. This fact makes it increasingly difficult to create a perfect plan for everyone, when you consider that everyone is different, and everyone has a different way that they would like to build the business. This forces many plans to be more generic in how they pay, and allows the distributors to conform to the plan. This is necessary for you to be able to grow your business.

Many times there are leaders or associates who would like to have a special bonus based on parties held in their homes, internet recruiting, customer based promotions, etc. They would like special incentives for the way that *they* build, and often forget that the people they are getting through this process may want to build in a different way. Often times, these compensation plans that are designed for a specific building behavior or recruiting process fail in the long run, because it may compensate the loudest distributor, but it doesn't compensate the majority of their team.

For this reason, most plans should be designed for the majority, and be generic enough that multiple teams or leaders with multiple or opposite ways of building their business can both succeed and be profitable. Yet, there are also times when companies who may have had some previous experience with one direction of building will focus parts of their plan to internet recruiting bonuses, home party bonuses, or other types of behavior that may appeal to some, but not to all. Watch out for these companies and bonuses. This is usually a sure sign that the company, management, compensation plan team, or even leading distributors (who are usually the loudest about the plan) do not understand the dynamics of their plan, the industry, or the long-term consequences of their actions. This is a great window into whether the executive and corporate staff fully understand what they are doing.

DISTRIBUTOR CHANGES

This is *almost* a standard rule: In most circumstances do not try to change the compensation plan as a distributor.

Hopefully, with just the few comments that have been made, it has become a little bit clearer that compensation plans are more complex than most people believe. Beyond anything that is mentioned here in this text, the full complexity of a good plan cannot be expressed in such a small text as is presented here. Although compensation plans are designed to compensate, they are also designed to create behavior in a distributor force – that is where the largest complexity comes about. The attempt to create behavior with a plan sometimes has nothing to do with the finances of the plan or how you get paid – but how you perceive you will be paid, and how you view your own parameters in the plan. There have been countless times that I have met with people who only see one side of the equation and request changes – but until they have also seen the numbers, the psychology of behavior in an incentive-based environment, and the goals of the distributor field as a whole, they cannot comprehend the full consequence of their request.

Remember, that when you change the plan for one person, you are changing it for a whole population of people. The majority of the time, when requests come to change a plan, they are coming through the eyes and experiences of one person who is looking for one result, and has only experienced a single behavior in a limited population of the whole organization. Even when they attempt to look through the eyes of the whole, they are still shaded by their personal experiences, and it is hard to relate to the other distributors in the field who may or may not agree with the changes. As stated in the previous section, the compensation plan always needs to be made for the majority – and to some degree that needs to be respected.

With that said, are there times when the company gets it all wrong and should change the plan?

YES! There are many times, and I see compensation plans everyday that are disastrous, and are in desperate need to be overhauled. But, if you firmly believe that you see a plan that needs to change, and it needs to change enough that you want to go and fight for the change with the company – then what does that say about the company's management team and their real experience in the industry and their ability to succeed in a market that is getting more and more competitive every single day? I would suggest that if you see such a plan, your energies could be spent finding a better plan for you somewhere else, than trying to change the current plan you are in.

Regardless, there will be times when someone (usually a larger leader) will fight for a change in the plan, and this is usually wrought with agenda. If a leader of an organization boasts that he has done the impossible and changed the plan "for the good of the company", I would watch out for that as well. The plan may now be enhanced a bit, but what does that still say about the executive team of the company who needed to change the plan to begin with, or one that would yield to a distributor who may, or may not, have the best interest in mind for the whole of the company? This is true particularly if you do not fully agree with this leader's direction in how they build – because you can be sure that the leader swayed these changes to benefit his personal growth and organization.

CHANGES VS. ADJUSTMENTS

As stated above, there are times when compensation plans need *changing*, and then again, there are times when they just need *adjusting*. It is important to note the difference between these two actions, as well as the potential consequences.

When a compensation plan changes significantly it is usually a sign of need. This usually indicates that the previous plan was not working, by either paying too much or not incentivizing the desired behavior correctly. The majority of the time it is out of need, because it was ill-conceived and not a stable plan. A full compensation plan change also shows lack of leadership in the organization, both in the field and in the corporate office. If the company was not successful before the change, making the risky move of a compensation plan change can devastate any organization, and can demolish anything struggling.

A compensation plan change can redirect the entire dynamics of the organization and how it grows. It can intimidate currently active members of your team and can threaten your current check, not only in how it is calculated, but also in how it can change behavior and spur emotion. This level of change can, and should, also reflect in all of the indirect products that are offered, particularly the management team of the company. The main take away from the current discussion is that a complete compensation plan change is not a good sign for anyone.

With that said, there are types of product companies that are less affected by these changes. If the company is a unique-product company, and the compensation plan is really only a byproduct (not an indirect product) of people genuinely using the product, then even drastic changes can still be made with relative safety. At the end of the day, everyone will still buy the product because it is unique, and it shouldn't adjust the cost of the product, which for these people is the most important thing.

Adjusting the plan is slightly different and can happen for a number of reasons. When you adjust the plan you make more subtle changes to the plan that might include the way a bonus is calculated, the percentage paid in a particular bonus, or a small adjustment to rank qualifications. These can sometimes be innocent and highly beneficial to the company.

When adjustments happen in the plan, the most important thing to evaluate, in order to determine how significant of a plan change it is, is to ask "Why this change took place?" If the adjustment took place because it needed to pay less in a particular bonus, that is not a good sign. Those types of problems can usually be identified with a good degree of analysis before a compensation plan is launched, and a change in the total payout, in order to save the company financially or the stability of the plan, shows that this research was either not done or was ignored when the company first launched the plan. This also can speak volumes about the company in a negative way.

There are times when an adjustment will be made that will actually benefit the distributor significantly. These are usually when the company realizes that they are not paying enough to the distributor force to have a competitive compensation plan, and they will up the percentages or add some bonuses in order to increase behavior and total compensation to the field.

Small adjustments can also be a sign of a maturing compensation plan. As companies grow, compensation plans also change in their behavior slightly and their dynamics. There are many times that when the company hits $100+ million, bonuses that were highly effective at the beginning of the company are not effective now because of the way they are maximized, and there may have to be some subtle adjustments to correct behavior, because that bonus is now behaving different as a result of the size of the company. These types of changes can be natural, and if done properly, should be able to almost go unnoticed by the distributor force, or increase the distributor's excitement for the plan because that bonus wasn't paying anyone anyway (and eventually was seen as a loss of potential funds). One of the most talented skills a company can acquire is a good manager over the compensation plan that can implement subtle changes without anyone noticing – and this is an art more than anything else.

In most cases, complete compensation plan changes and adjustments can be seen as a window into the lack of experience and qualities that you need in the company you choose. If they are significant changes, you also need to be concerned that they still may not have it right, and they may change it again in the future. Yet, even with all of that said, there are times when small and subtle adjustments are necessary, safe, and smart, as long as they are implemented with minimal recognition from the field.

The Easy Fallacy

Most people in today's society have been trained to look for the "get-rich-quick" approach, and unfortunately, there are network marketing companies who are trying to fill that void. Most distributors all want an easy way to make money. They are always looking for the easiest and most lucrative compensation plan. This is not unique, nor is there anything inherently wrong with this. This is something that is natural in the human being: wanting something good as cheaply and as easily as possible.

Everyone is looking for the easiest way to make the most amount of money, and many companies advertise the ease that they offer and the ability for you to make more money than you can imagine. These are not good. Keep your eye out for anything that says you do not need to work to make money in their company.

Just the other day, I was watching a new marketing campaign by a new industry rocket (shoot up quickly, but sure to fall just as fast), and their campaign was direct in saying that you didn't need to work to make money from them. This is a fraud and a lie of life – and in any circumstance that it might be true, it is just as dangerous.

Network Marketing is hard work, and the more someone works, the more someone will make in this industry – that is a fact. When you hear that anything will be easy, it should send up red flags, and require further investigation. Often times, these companies are only trying to get your money, not trying to help you earn money – and once you have purchased your product, they have completed their transaction and are done with you. You then find yourself in the same situation that was described in the first chapter, and more than likely, will be bitter towards the industry for the rest of your life. There is no such thing as a free ride.

Yet, there are times when companies design their compensation plans to be a little easier to generate a degree of success and income without much effort. These are also extremely dangerous. The easier it is to earn an income worth being excited about, the easier it is to have it taken away. Remember, there is only so much money that can go around each transaction, and it is just as easy for everyone else to make the same amount of money that you are making. This means that there is quick and significant growth, because people want to make money; but there comes a point when the company can no longer afford to pay the promised amount of money, and requires a change in their plan – which is sure to take nearly everything that you have come to expect in earnings away from you.

Sadly, these actions are often planned from the very beginning of a company. Some companies will internally decide to launch with an extremely unstable plan with the hopes of generating a significant amount of revenue in a short period of time. They then can pay their investors back, make a great amount in return, and then change the plan, realizing that they already got out what they wanted, and anything that remains after such a change is icing on the cake. These are companies that are not worried about your business as much as their pockets, and they will never be there for the long haul.

If these plans are able to succeed, it ultimately limits the amount that even the hardest working leaders can earn. If everyone can earn $500 in a plan, than eventually, the only way to make the plan stable is to limit the most anyone can make to $500 or less. Even the hardest working people make less money in these plans, and the business eventually corrodes from the top down.

These companies also do much more harm than good in the industry. These companies not only help give the industry a bad name, but they create an expectation among people that they can make money, and that they should make money without any effort. These associates believe this because for a short while, they do make money, and then it is taken away. This leaves them looking for the next opportunity, but no other company can compete with that concept, and cannot give them what they are looking for. These companies not only do the industry a great injustice, but they give false impressions to those who they capture.

PAYOUT BALANCE

Common sense dictates that the more money that goes out into the field, the more money the distributors will earn. This is often true, but can sometimes leads distributors to wish for a much higher payout percentage in the plan. They wish that instead of giving only 50% to the field, they want 75% to the field. As discussed previously, there is only so much money that can go around, and there is a fine balance between giving the distributors a real opportunity to make a significant income, pricing the product with a marketable price point, and keeping the corporate environment afloat to help support your business. As a general rule, if you notice that someone is offering 60% + in commissions, there are a number of questions you should ask.

Is the corporate environment able to stay afloat with less than 40%? Remember that the company needs to pay for the cost of producing the product, the staff to help service your company, as well as the infrastructure, not only to maintain, but to grow the company. At the end of the day, you need the corporate environment to thrive in order for you to have the opportunity to grow. Also, at the end of the day, if the corporate team is selling enough product but not making enough to stay afloat, it may dictate a compensation plan change that will negatively adjust your expected earnings.

Is the product competitively priced in the industry, and are you paying too much for your product? If the company can stay afloat with the low percentage it keeps, it may be because they have increased the price of the product significantly enough to change their revenue to cover their costs. This can mean the product is not competitively priced for the market place, which can make it extremely difficult to build your business, or that you are paying too much for your product, because it could be

93

priced much less. A standard rule is for every 5% in commissions, it affects 10% of the total cost to the end consumer.

POPULATION VOLUME VS. SALES VOLUME

As it has been said before, you only make money from the sales volume that takes place in your organization. If you want more money, then it is reasonable to expect that you go and find more sales, and therefore will make more money. Yet, there is another aspect to this equation. That is, that in order for you to generate sales volume, you need to have a population of people under you in the organization.

The reason this needs to be considered when you are trying to determine which company is right for you is that you should be able to evaluate both the product price point, together with the compensation plan, and determine whether the population of people necessary to generate the desired check is feasible or even possible.

For instance, in most compensation plans, we could guess that the residual income will generally be about 5% of the commissionable volume within the organizations. This means that if you want to make a $1,000, you will need to produce about 20,000 CV in sales within your networking organization. (Keep in mind that this is only an example for you to better understand the concept – you could make more, or you could make less.)

Now let's say that your product is a product that carries 100 CV a case (of juice). This means that you need to have a population of 200 people in your team, all ordering a case to generate that 20,000 CV, which gives you your $1,000 check.

Now let's say that your product is a smaller product designed to be affordable for everyone, and carries 10 CV an order (of lip balm). This means that you need to have a population of

2,000 people in your team, all ordering, in order to generate that same 20,000 CV, which yields your $1,000 earnings.

Now you need to compare the two populations of needed people. With one product, you need to have 200 people, and with another, you need to find 2,000 people. Now it might be true that you may be able to find more people with a more affordable product, but can you find 10 times more people? With more or less effort?

The answer to these questions are not obvious, because they are different for each person, but this idea still must be considered in order for you to be more fully aware of what will be expected or required for you to reach the desired goals for your income. Knowing this may not change your decision on the company you choose, but it may mean that you adjust your business plan to accommodate the required population needed. Remember, you are not just trying to sell product and generate sales (or commissionable) volume, you are trying to find people who will do the same thing, and create a population which will create that sales volume.

SALES VOLUME VS. PRODUCT (COMMISSIONABLE) VOLUME

When analyzing the percentage of commissions that is paid back out to the distributor, one thing that you will want to keep in mind is the discrepancy between the actual sales cost and the Product or Commissionable Volume that is associated with the product or service. A compensation plan may boast a higher percentage of payout, but you must keep in mind that this percentage is usually not calculated on the Sales Volume or the amount the product costs the end consumer, but on the Commissionable Volume.

Commissionable or Product Volume is the amount of product credit the distributor gets for the sale of a particular product, and is not necessarily associated with the end price of the product. For example, the average popular network marketing "functional beverage" (juice) may cost $130 a case, but may only give 100 points in Commissionable Volume. This means that for every $130 that you sell, you really only get credit for 100 points of volume in that transaction, and that boasted percentage of commissions is calculated off that number.

Now, I am not saying that this is a bad thing. Some companies use this to distribute a really great product while being able to keep it within a marketable price point for the end consumer. These products, if they were priced with the sales amount and the commissionable volume to be equal, would require an additional $10 to the end consumer for every additional $5 sent back into the field for distributor commissions. This discrepancy between the sales price and Commissionable Volume is sometimes a great tool to ensure that good quality products can still be affordable.

This also is an area that obviously can be abused, which is why it is important to be aware of these discrepancies. Some companies will boast a high percentage of payout (calculated on the commissionable volume), but then they will adjust the difference between the sales price and the commissionable volume significantly. The wider this gap is, the greater this tool is being manipulated and negatively affecting your commissions.

A good general rule of thumb is not to accept more than a 20% difference. For every $100, make sure you are getting at least 80 points in commissionable volume. If you are getting more than this, that is also not a bad thing, just ensure that the product is still priced to be marketable. If you are getting less than this, be weary of the company – they are more than likely hoping that you will not notice.

Here is an example to show what is actually going out in the field from the sales volume amount (I will use the juice example above in the parenthesis). Take the amount of percentage advertised to pay back out to the field (let's say 50%), and multiply that into the amount of Commissionable Volume given for that particular product (100CV). This will tell you how much money will go back out into the field for each unit sold ($50). Now divide that amount of money into the amount of money it costs to purchase the product at wholesale ($130), and you will get the percentage of actual sales that are returned to the distributors (38.46%). Remember, you want to know this number because the more money that goes out to the field, the larger your check can be for the same amount of work. If the same company offered 5% extra to the field for the same product and the same marketable price point, it would be fair to say that it would have a positive effect upon your check.

BREAKAGE

Breakage is also something that can directly affect your check, but often goes unnoticed, because it is never included in any compensation plan literature and is often only an internal discussion among the Executive Teams within these companies.

Breakage is arguably the most important part of the plan, or at least being able to identify it. This is defined as money that is budgeted, advertised, or marketed to be paid out in the plan, but is not (for a number of potential reasons). This is when a company says that they could pay out 50% (or more) of commissions, but really they are only paying out 30% or 40%. This is the case for 98% of all network marketing companies.

This is also reasonably legal, and therefore, happens much more often than distributors would like to believe. All the company is saying is that they *can* pay up to 50%, and that "can" means that if everything in the company worked out just perfectly, and everyone enrolled the right amount of people, mathematically speaking the compensation plan could (hypothetically) pay out that number. What happens though is much different. Not everyone that enrolls engages like everyone else, and not everyone hits their ranks when they could or should. This is called *breakage behavior* – where the behavior of the distributors creates financial breakage in the compensation plan.

What happens then is that money is left on the table, money that could have been earned (in a hypothetical situation), but is not being earned by anyone. This money that never goes out to the field stays in the company, is called breakage, and is additional revenue for the company. It is fair to say that if this additional revenue were placed back into the field, that the distributors would have larger checks, and would have made more money. Yet, breakage is not the enemy, not understanding that breakage exists, or being able to identify how much could exist in a particular plan affects your ability to identify a lucrative plan over a non-competitive plan. Breakage has been part of every network marketing company for the entire history of the industry, up until just the last ten years – so some of the most stable plans that have been around and lasted the test of time all had breakage. So, as much as it is not the enemy, after the last ten years, those plans are now far less competitive.

It is critical to be able to identify these types of plans. This identification can happen rather easily by asking the right questions. Here are two simple questions that help to bring out whether there is breakage, and if you are lucky, how much breakage is in the plan: (1) If this bonus or level was not qualified for, who gets that money? (2) Is there anything that absorbs breakage and redirects it back into the field?

These are great questions. Identify a bonus or level that may be earned at the highest ranks. Simply point at that bonus and ask, where does that money go if I don't qualify to reach that far (or anyone for that matter)? If the answer to that question is, no one gets it – then the real answer is that the company gets it, and it is breakage.

In contrast, sometimes breakage will be present in a plan, but there will be additional bonuses that are designed to absorb that breakage and pay it out in another fashion. Asking whether there is such a bonus is critical. You may not need to fully understand how it works, but a sure sign is that it will be a fluctuation payout, because the breakage will be fluctuating from commission period to commission period.

Remember, the more money that is paid out to the field, the larger the checks are, and in order for that to be correct, it needs to really be paid out (not just marketed).

There are also additional forms of breakage that you need to be aware of. Unfortunately, they are nearly impossible for you to be able to identify that these forms are present in a company. The most prevalent form of non-traditional breakage is *corporate-induced breakage.* This is when the company creates a compensation plan that is designed not to have breakage, but then they may place a position in the tree to capture a check and come right back to the company. This is by definition breakage – money that is designed to go out to the field that is going back into the company. This is why learning as much as you can about the executive team is also important.

EXECUTIVE TEAM

Learning all you can about who is running the company can be critical to the longevity of your home-based business, which is why there is a whole chapter of things to keep in mind when reviewing your executive team. They also can have a direct impact on your commissions as well.

Not only can the executive team create breakage if they want to, they can also make additional deals with leaders that, at the end of the day, can change your check. There are many executive teams that try to build the companies distributor force by partnering up with other larger leaders in other companies. These executive teams then try to sway them to the company, and to bring their whole organization along with them. In an effort to bring them over to the company, they will make additional deals on the side for additional commissions to flow to these leaders for their building activity. These are the closest things to bribes you will find in the industry. The question that is then posed is, "Who is paying for these leaders?" The company usually cannot afford to pay out-of-pocket for these leaders, so they take the money they need to fund these deals out of the commission engine and the total amount that goes out to the regular distributor force. The executive team can often justify such actions because, at the end of the day, in their mind, this is a "commission".

This means that when a new big leader shows up in your company that seems to have brought a whole team with them from another company, the money that is funding that deal came out of your check. This leader and the company are now profiting, using money that you would have earned, and are now not earning. In an indirect way, you paid for that leader and, more than likely, you are not benefiting from that leader.

Sadly, the only way to really know if any of this questionable activity is taking place is to really know your executive team – which is really hard to do. But there are some things to that you can consider. If your executive team seems to be really leader-minded, is able to relate well to them, and seems to naturally draw leaders to them, it is less likely that they will need to ever pay for leaders. If the company seems to be struggling, and then all of a sudden a leader pops up with a whole team, there is usually something going on.

The type of executive team that you have running the company ultimately has the last say when it comes to approving commissions. There are even times when they themselves may have positions in the tree designed to capture a portion of that promised commission percentage. The problem is you can never tell 100% who is and who isn't going to behave that way. I have seen some of the most ethical men eventually cave in to such temptation as to messing with the commission engine to maximize revenue, capture additional funds, or even pay for employees using positions in the tree.

It is also important to note that not everyone in the industry has this problem, but it is out there and so, for the sake of your own commissions, you may want to study your executive team and be aware who you are working with.

MANAGEMENT OF THE PLAN

There is probably 5% of the industry (including corporate and independent associates) that can really understand plans, and they all believe they know and fully understand plans in the full spectrum. But out of all my travels, for every 100 people who believe strongly that they know compensation plans enough to build, manage or make valuable suggestions; only 1 *may* be able to actually aid in the management of a plan. It is difficult to find someone who has experience with leaders, standard home-business associates, commission data management, an understanding of the psychology of incentives, and the financial understanding of the corporate environment to really be able to aid in the development and management of a compensation plan.

It is equally difficult to try to train someone in all these areas, as the educator needs to be one of these highly experienced individuals, and the learner needs to be just as interested in developing his skills. Being a compensation plan "guru" is really an art, more than a skill, and continually needs attention and practice in new analysis.

This is all mentioned because the management of the plan can make all the difference in how successful the plan will be. Who is managing the plan and the experience that they carry can make the difference in whether the executive team makes the right decisions on their recommendations. It can affect how regularly and on-time commission payments are made and how clear the compensation plan training will be.

If the company does not have the right management of the plan, then the literature may be wrong, the calculations may be wrong, and the compensation plan or any changes and adjustments to the plan may not be analyzed, calculated, and evaluated enough to safely justify their implementation. A similar lesson I have learned from every company I have worked with that didn't have a Commissions Department to audit the literature, payouts, and the process is that these companies *will* have the wrong literature, *will* have the wrong calculations on their commission payouts, and *will* make significant errors in bonus logic and adjustments that will risk both the distributors earning and the longevity of the company.

Charismatic leaders will have ideas to change the plan, executive members will desperately try to increase sales, and everyone and their dog will have "improvements" on the plan - and who they are presenting those ideas to and their experience in analysis and distributor behavior makes all the difference in making these ideas work or turning them down gracefully. If there is no one there to manage the plan, then there is no one there to make anything work – and it is very rare that these "improvements" will work. Even the best ideas in the industry wouldn't have worked in their original form without someone to walk through the process and improve the improvements in implementations and functionality.

Be familiar with who is managing the Commissions Department, who is running their engine, and the experience of the programmers or software providers that are programming their commission engine.

COMPETITIVE PAYOUT DEFINITIONS

As previously mentioned, there are many plans that say they pay one amount, and yet do not pay anywhere close to it. After reviewing the previous sections that affect the actual payout, it is about time that we address what the term *competitive* really means.

On average, each company proposes to pay something around 50%. Out of all those standard claims, 80% of those companies will really pay less than 30%, and will not at all be considered competitive. Fifteen percent will pay between 30-40%, and still not be considered competitive. Four percent of the industry will really pay above 40% of their sales, and these are considered competitive plans. Less than one percent will pay above 45% of their sales and be considered extremely competitive.

Although it takes a very trained eye to be able to look at a plan and identify the true competiveness of it and the projected real payout, these numbers will be evident within the checks of the distributors.

Thoughts to take away from this chapter:
- There is usually a difference between the marketing of the plan and the reality of the plan.
- There is only so much money to go around.
- Literature is the gateway to understanding the plan and being able to evaluate the plan.
- Knowing more about the plan does not directly affect your commissions as much as working the plan.
- If you feel like you need to change the plan, you are probably in the wrong opportunity.
- Consider the various breakage potentials.
- Know your executive team and the management of the commission department.

CHAPTER 7

COMPENSATION PLANS: TYPES, STRUCTURES, AND STRATEGIES

Arguably, the compensation plan is the most used, if not important, indirect product that a network marketing company has to offer. Just like products, it is important to understand the different types of compensation plans and their benefits, culture, and how they fit within your personality.

Each compensation plan is based on a structure, and it is this structure that usually defines most of the culture and the building technique associated with that plan. It is also this general structure that defines what type of plan it is and how it will be marketed, sold, shared, and utilized. Oddly enough, these structures, even though they are the major undercurrent in the plan, do not define wealth or profitability. In fact, the bonuses that are usually tied to these structures are not the most lucrative in the plan, they just dictate the building behavior and requirements in how an organization grows. Some plans provide greater stability, and some more synergy, but at the end of the day, the harder you work in any plan, the more you will make from the plan.

With that being the case, it is still important to understand what type of structure the plan is and how you will be expected to build. It is equally important to investigate how that

SELECTING A NETWORK MARKETING OPPORTUNITY

will dictate your building strategies in your organization and how that will coincide with your personality and your abilities.

STRUCTURES

Although there are extensive variations to each of the bonuses, in the most basic of definitions, there are really three general structures that are widely available, and each structure has increasing enforced structure limitations: the unilevel (with minimal structure limitations), the binary (with a medium amount of structure limitation), and the matrix (with extremely high structure limitations). As a result, each structure has wide swings in the types of variations, their positive and negative attributes, their life spans, and their building strategies. The rest of this chapter is designed to walk through some basic rules and standards of each of the general structures for you to consider when selecting the network marketing opportunity for you.

UNILEVEL: THE DEFINITION

Unilevel is probably the most standard structure in the industry. This is where network marketing gets its casual name of Multi-Level Marketing. In the Unilevel, as you bring people into the organization, each one of your personally introduced (or sponsored) new associates are directly connected to you. This becomes your first level, and you are able to earn commissions on them and their activity; as your first level begins to enroll new associates themselves, that becomes their first level, and in turn, your second level. This pattern is followed as you begin to create multiple levels within your organization; each level being farther and farther removed from you in your genealogy but still connected. As you progress through the compensation plan (usually through the rank requirements), you are able to capture a degree or percentage of commissions from additional levels in your organization. This allows you to leverage on the work of others in your organization and increase your commissions by earning on more members of your team.

When it is said that the Unilevel has minimal enforced structural limitations, that is not to say that there are no requirements through the plan to help guide your building strategy. What it does mean is that in a Unilevel, there is nothing that is enforced inherently through the programming of how you *have* to build. Nothing will force you to build in a particular fashion in your genealogy or to shape your organization – although there may be positive or negative consequences in building in one pattern compared to another. In Unilevel plans, you are able to build your organization by building it wide through enrolling a lot of people personally (from one person to a million people on your first level), or deep (by helping others enroll and building deeper levels). In fact, a common saying when referring to building Unilevel organizations is that you are supposed to build wide if you are looking for profitability, but build deep if you are looking for stability. This would be a proven statement, and might go without saying, that inherently the distributor should strive for both.

The key to identifying a Unilevel structure within a compensation plan is going to be that they do not limit the amount of people that can be placed directly to you within the organization, with that being classified as your first level.

UNILEVEL: VARIATIONS (COMPRESSION)

There are some variations in any type of compensation plan that is inherent in the concept of the compensation plan itself. These are things like rank qualifications, additional bonuses associated with the compensation plan, and other unique aspects. Although these are variations, they are variations within all plans, and are generally independent of the structure of the plan.

In Unilevel plans, there is one variation that directly affects the structure, building technique and profitability of the compensation plan. The major variation in Unilevel plans is known as Compression. As you build your Unilevel organization, you will discover that some people will not be as active as others and that they will take up a space in your organization, or even worse, stand between you and a more profitable level within your team. Compression is the way that the plan compensates for that type of activity (or lack of activity within your team), and allows you to move passed any less active associates to qualify and earn commissions on more active associates and, therefore, increasing your profitability. Compression is necessary in all Unilevel plans to even make it financially functional.

There are three general types of compression that are used in Unilevel Plans: Standard Compression, Dynamic Compression (Original), and "Compressed" Dynamic Compression (an *attempted* enhancement). It is important to understand that although sometimes a company may use the terminology in their plan of one form of compression, they can sometimes be using a different form of compression to appear more marketable. This is why it is important for you to understand what happens in all three types of compression and some of the behavior that follows. This way, you can determine independently from what the company says, what the company is actually doing.

The reason why I attempt to make this such a strong point is an experience I had in one of my early consulting jobs. I was working for some friends on a new compensation plan for their company. They had chosen a Unilevel plan, and I learned pretty quickly that they were extremely interested in having as much breakage back to the company as they could get, but they wanted marketability as well. So when the discussion around what type of compression to use started, I learned that there wasn't much conversation at all. They had already decided to use Standard Compression (a form that generally gives more breakage to the company), but in their literature, claimed Dynamic Compression (a form that generally creates less breakage to the company). They were able to do this, because there really is no governing text in the industry defining these terms, and no Attorney General really understands this terminology enough to challenge this type of marketing fraud. After some rather heated discussions concerning the ethics of this action, I learned rather quickly that it would probably be best for me not to extend my contract with that company. This experience also gave me the motivation to research the entire industry and compile the most commonly used terms to create the test *Industry Standard: Network Marketing Terms, Definitions, and Glossary* in an attempt to help standardize these terms.

Standard Compression

Standard Compression is the simplest to understand and is more universally used. Simply put, in Standard Compression, when there is an empty spot in regard to a commissionable order in one level created by a distributor's inactivity, or lack of order, the next level under that person will compress up to that position.

An example of this would be if you signed up your grandma, and she didn't order this month. Well, if there is anyone that she signed up that did order, those orders would compress up into your grandma's position, and you would earn commission on those orders as if they were in that level. The end result of this type of compression is that if you are qualifying for ten levels of Unilevel pay with standard compression, you may actually be able to earn commissions from 12-15 levels of your organization. Standard Compression decreases breakage to the company in comparison to having no compression, but only decreases the breakage slightly.

Dynamic Compression (Original)

The original Dynamic Compression changes the way volume or orders are paid out in the Unilevel. Instead of paying from the qualifying member down, Dynamic Compression looks from the order and pays up the tree a number of times. If there are nine levels that could be paid out in the compensation plan, then each order tries to pay out nine times up the tree. The Commission Engine takes the order and looks up to see who qualifies for the first level (or in other words who qualified to have it paid out the first time). After it is paid out the first time (or level), it looks further up the tree for a second level, and then a third, and so on. In this process, if it is paid out five times and needs to skip twenty people to find the next person who qualified for a sixth level, it does so.

This type of Dynamic Compression maximizes the payout of the leaders, while minimizing the breakage to the company. If the plan has fixed percentage payouts, this type of compression does not eliminate breakage; it only minimizes the breakage, but does a very good job of it. In compensation plans that may have a fluctuating percentage based on breakage, this type of compression can entirely eliminate breakage. Either way, this type of compression yields the most fair and balanced checks for the leaders, and helps them fairly reach deep into their organization, and is therefore, the most sought after.

One leader that I was close to was qualifying for nine levels of dynamic compression, but was only using 6 of them, and was still capturing on 32 levels of their organization (all the way to the bottom of the whole team)!

"Compressed" Dynamic Compression (attempted enhancement)

This is one type of compression where it is critical to understand what it does in order to determine what actually is taking place in a compensation plan. This is most commonly mislabeled as the original Dynamic Compression, but does very different things and affects the organization significantly.

In an effort to eliminate breakage, some companies tried to enhance Dynamic Compression. This action yielded an unfairly distributed payout to the field, although with the right buzz words, it can make it marketable to some and give the appearance of competitiveness to others.

This enhancement gives multiple levels of dynamic compression to one person. So, if in the engine, you were going to be paid the third time on an order but qualified for five levels, this type of Dynamic Compression would compress all those levels (three, four, and five) into your check, and the next person to earn commissions would need to qualify for six levels. This type of compression had its hay day, and people thought this was a great evolution. Sadly, they were wrong.

What happened when these plans eventually matured is that the leaders at the top of the tree were not reaching into their organization any more as a result of this dynamic compression. They were actually reaching less than in standard compression. Their teams were starting to qualify for higher levels, and the leaders who helped build the organization were finding themselves with no Unilevel pay as compression was giving all the commissions to their downline members, leaving nothing for them to earn. This eventually leaves these companies leaderless

– as it is very profitable for the short run, but fails to give significant residual income for the long run.

Compression is important in a Unilevel compensation plan, and some type of compression is necessary. Standard Compression can be okay if it is a product-based company and there is a lucrative back end of bonuses – but it still wouldn't be seen as competitive, as standard compression pretty much ensures that there is a good degree of breakage. The "Compressed" Dynamic Compression may minimize breakage and have the appearance of marketability, but creates an extremely unstable environment for a company to grow on – and is recommended to stay away from. The original Dynamic Compression is a fair balance, and it could be said that it is necessary in order to create a Unilevel plan that would be competitive. The Original Dynamic Compression decreases breakage significantly (if not altogether with the potential options in their bonus structure), helps the leaders continue to reach deep into their organization for the long haul, and constantly distributes the commissions fairly among the qualifying team members.

UNILEVEL: THE PROS

Unilevel Compensation Plans are sometimes touted as the most ethical plans. This is seen by some because your team grows on your own activity, and therefore, your success is seen more as your ability, and less your upline team member's ability to grow your organization. This play on words is most likely to be seen coming from companies and associates who are already in Unilevel structures and feel less free to move from them. Remember, compensation plans are much like products, and when someone is sold on one type of plan, sometimes they need to be convicted towards that type of organization or indirect product in order to feel good about the decision that they made.

To be fair, in some regards, they are right. Unilevel plans do show a stronger networking skill, and are often much more successful with product-focused companies. These are also sometimes the easiest plan to understand and teach. As long as they at least have the original Dynamic Compression, they can be profitable plans as well. The Unilevel plans give some network marketing traditionalists the feeling of comfort, as the original idea of how network marketing was "supposed to be".

UNILEVEL: THE CONS

These are sometimes the hardest plans to sell. The same points that make the Unilevel plan seen as the most ethical plans are also seen as what make these plans not appeal to others. Sure, Unilevel plans are more a gauge of your own abilities, but who wants to gauge their own abilities when their upline could be helping? In comparison to other types of plans, the Unilevel plan requires less support from your upline or sponsor, and therefore, associates are often less likely to get that support. There is nothing inherent in the Unilevel plan that requires that the sponsor or upline help build your team in any fashion whatsoever. This creates a lot of individual teams and less synergy in an organization; as a result, this can create less marketability and less retention in the long run.

UNILEVEL: THE LIFESPAN

The lifespan of these types of plans are very good, as long as they get off the ground. These are long-lasting plans because everything can be budgeted and predicted rather well. The compensation that flows from these plans can often be predictable to the distributors as well.

As these are easier to budget for, there is less concern from the corporate environment that the plan will be over budget, or if handled properly, that they will ever need to change the compensation plan. These plans can be created, audited, analyzed and done right the first time, every time. There is little surprise both to the distributor field and to the corporate staff. These are also easier to manage internally, and can usually be done relatively cheaply with a very small team – even for a large company. They are safe, long-term, and stable.

But this lifespan analysis is all dependent upon the company's ability to get off the ground. With the Unilevel being less marketable than other plan structures, there is increasing difficulty in getting new companies with these Unilevel structures to be financially viable. For companies that create and develop a degree of success with these plans (in spite of the plan) will have a good chance of having a compensation plan with the lifespan described above.

UNILEVEL: THE BUILDING STRATEGIES

The building strategies change slightly, depending upon the difference variations in the types of compression detailed above; another reason to understand the compression within a compensation plan.

If the compensation plan only offers standard compression, then the building strategy is to personally enroll as many people as you can. Keeping all of the enrollments and placements personally allows you to have a huge first level. At that point, you need to start incentivizing these first level members to engage and work on building their own teams. In this fashion, there no is synergy within your team, as you need to keep everyone to yourself (personally enrolled and placed). It is not wise to give away enrollments or placements in this circumstance that may reasonably be yours. As you can see, this is a rather cut throat approach – but if that is what your compensation plan offers, that is exactly what they are teaching your to do. At the end of the day, this directs you to build your organization wide and shallow. Shallow organizations are not safe or stable for the long haul, but this is the only way to maximize your earnings with standard compression. Your hope is that you will be lucky and find someone as dedicated to their own success as you are to yours, and you may be able to develop some depth with the leadership that you enroll or develop. Developing leadership through personal development within your team is really your only chance of building depth, as you should not structurally build their team for them – all the while hoping that the application of your training will encourage their own organization to grow deep.

If the company offers the original Dynamic Compression, then your building strategy is going to be quite different. Instead of building wide and shallow, your entire goal is to build deep. If you have the ability to retain the enrollment credit (for fast-start bonuses), but give the placement of the enrollment to someone else, that is exactly what you do. In this circumstance, you actually build straight lines down, enrolling new members and placing them deeper and deeper in your organization. You may want to do this through a few lines, depending on the amount of lines you will need for your rank qualifications. What this does is create synergy and excitement from your team as you are building more and more people underneath them (in a straight line). Because everyone is in a straight line, they will be qualifying for some commissions off these people, but not all, unless they themselves engage in the organization, build other lines, and qualify for more depth in what you have built under them. What this also does with the original Dynamic Compression (as long as you are high ranking yourself), is that it allows you to still capture commissions on the depth of your organization, regardless of how deep.   By building in a straight line, you are creating synergy and excitement, and as long as you are qualifying for your rank, you can reach all that volume even if it is thirty to a hundred levels down, just as if it was only two levels down. This strategy gives you higher retention, higher excitement, and therefore, duplication from your team, and keeps your profitability high while creating a more stable organization.

If the company offers the enhanced approach of "Compressed" Dynamic Compression, you do not want to build deep, as you eventually will be cut off from your depth. You will want to continue to build shallow and wide, and attempt to qualify for the highest rank possible to allow you to capture more levels of your own organization. In these circumstances, do not expect to get any support from your upline in helping you qualify, as it will not benefit them if you ever out-rank them.

Binary: The Definition

The term "Binary" refers to two. The easiest way to explain a binary is that each business center (or distributor) has two teams, a left team and a right team.   As the distributor enrolls someone new, they will place them in one of those two teams. Equally, everyone that you enroll and place among those two teams will also have two teams of their own that they will be trying to build. As you place more people in one of your teams, you also are inherently placing the new enrollments also within one of the two teams of someone in your organization. This is one reason why Binaries are famous. They are relatively simple to understand, yet they carry a sense of synergy and unity as your enrollments have the potential to help everyone in that particular team.

Binaries are relatively structured, more so than Unilevel, but less than a Matrix; you are required to have two teams, and you cannot have more than two teams, but you do have the freedom to place new enrollments anywhere within those teams.

Within the binary structure, there are a few variations to be aware of that will dictate how the binary structures will payout. The binary will be the way the structure must be built, but the type of binary will determine how you will get paid on that structure. The different variations can be detailed with the general labels of: The Cycle Binary, The Weak Leg Binary, The Business Center Binary, and the Hybrid Binary.

The Cycle Binary

The Cycle Binary is one of the most difficult binaries to manage; at the end of the day, it will usually either pay too much and need adjusting, or it won't pay enough and need adjusting. It is extremely difficult to keep a good balance on a cycle binary in order to make it a long-term and stable compensation plan.

The cycle binary is called that because is pays on the creation of each cycle of volume within the binary structure. Simply put, there is a pre-defined volume ratio between the two teams that will be classified as a single cycle. These cycle definitions are determined by the company, and will vary from company to company. An example of each cycle would be when a company defines the cycle as a 500/1000 cycle. This means that every time you have 500 in commissionable volume in one leg, and 1000 in commissionable volume in the other leg, you have just created a cycle. Now, for each cycle you create each commission period, you will get a predetermined amount of money. This amount is also determined by the company and will fluctuate from company to company as well. To continue the example, if you have 1500 in volume in your left team for the week and 4000 in your right team, with the same 500/1000 cycle definitions, and each cycle being worth $50, you would have three cycles using 1500 of your left volume and 3000 of your right volume, which would be worth a total of $150.

Cycle binaries are unique, but they are also sometimes difficult to follow. Just like every other variation in every compensation plan, cycle binaries have some advantages and some disadvantages. One advantage is that for the hard-core marketers, they are able to bias their activity within some of their strong legs that they normally would need to avoid working with in other binaries. Some disadvantages for the cycle binaries are that it can be difficult for the unskilled networker to understand, and therefore, decreased effective duplication for the masses; some say it can overcomplicate the training of the compensation plan.

The major concern or worry with the cycle binary compensation plan is its internal management and the inability to make sure that this type of plan is stable. Too often it will pay way too much because of the behavior it creates, or it can be stingy in the value of each cycle, and therefore, doesn't pay enough. To add complications, when a cycle binary is too stingy and they increase the per cycle value, it actually changes the behavior in the field so much that it then risks overpaying. A common theme in network marketing consultants in the compensation plan arena is that if the cycle binary is paying just enough, it is paying too much, because it will eventually change the behavior. These things are monsters to manage (both internally and for the distributor field), and therefore, will eventually be changed.

The Weak Leg Binary

In the Weak Leg Binary, your pay is not determined by a cycle, but is determined by the amount of volume in your weaker leg. This means that whatever volume you have in the weaker of the two legs will determine what you earnings are in the binary. For example, if it is a 10% of the weaker leg plan, and you have 8,000 in volume in one leg and 12,000 in volume in another, then you would earn 10% of the 8,000, equaling $800.

Although it is classified as a different type of binary, these are actually very similar to the cycle binaries, except they require a much more balanced and stable approach. This really means that it is a 100/100 cycle, with each cycle valued a $10. You only get paid on what is balanced between the two legs.

These have become extremely popular in that they are simple to teach, simple to duplicate, and simple to calculate for most people.

The Business Center Binary

The Business Center Binaries often times are not going to be seen as a different types of binary to some people. This is because they can be paid out in various ways, but regardless of the way they pay the binary, the fact that it is a Business Center Binary defines the way you maximize your earnings. Business Center Binaries are call such because you are able to buy or qualify to command multiple business centers within the tree organization. These business centers can be offered in multiple ways. They can be offered and given to the leader who qualifies. They can be placed above the earlier business center, below the earlier business center, or even in an entirely different place in the tree. The business centers can be purchased through the compensation plan at the initial enrollment, or they can be purchased at any time. They can pay via the cycle binary model or the standard binary model; the key with the Multiple Business Center approach to the compensation plan is that you NEED multiple business centers in order to earn anything of significance with the plan. Some plans may offer multiple business centers, but they are not necessary in order to generate significant income, and therefore, are not classified as a Business Center Binary. The key is the NEED for more business centers to maximize the plan.

Historically, as binaries were first introduced to the industry, there was a fear that developed within the companies that were considering them that they were risking their companies on this new idea. Statistically speaking, the binary structure has the potential to pay outrageous amounts – much higher than any company could consider affording. These numbers created a great degree of risk, and those possible statistics are still true today. But what allows binary compensation plans to be safe is the human element and the impossibility that any group of human beings will create the perfect structure to maximize the plan (legitimately). This is what they call human breakage – in that no realistic human activity could create a circumstance where there would be no breakage. Yet, when binaries first came on the scene, they knew the statistics that revealed their liability, but they really didn't know the human element and the real behavior they could expect, because they had no good data to predict that behavior at that date. So, in order to move forward with the idea, they did the best thing they could think of, and that was limit the amount each business center could earn in the binary. This was a very wise idea at the time in that it minimized their risk and gave the industry an opportunity to see what was really going to happen.

When they limited the earning potential of a business center, they pushed it really low – only to a couple thousand dollars. This meant that once a leader built an organization to a couple thousand dollars of commissions, they were done – unless they were allowed to build an additional business center. And so was born the additional business center approach.

Multiple Business Center Plans was a very safe and wise way to introduce the Binary structure into the network marketing industry, but as the years of data was collected, it allowed other companies to confidently adjust the Binary options, and create much more marketable plans with long term stability.

In recent years, the Hybrid Binary has become popular, and many of them unnecessarily offer the multiple business center to their leader upline – these Hybrid plans (see below) are not considered Multiple Business Center Plans, because you do not need the additional centers to make additional money in the plan (in fact the additional business centers in those plans are nothing more than marketing).

The Hybrid Binary

As stated above, these have become extremely popular in the last few years, and although they really are not a different structure of binary, they are different enough to be mentioned here as a variation. The key to a Hybrid binary isn't what is happening in the binary, it is what is happening outside of the binary. In Hybrid Plans, the binary plan (whether a cycle or weak-leg plan) is only in the forefront for marketing, and it is paired up with high-paying backend bonuses related to a secondary structure. These high-paying bonuses can be anything from leadership pools, to a unilevel structure, and to additional incentives. These plans try (often times succeeding) to create the marketability of the binary using the synergy and unity that is inherent within it, and matching it up with a luctritive additional bonus structure (trying to create the best of both worlds). These can be extremely successful because they can market the easy-to-understand stuff to the general public, and get the big leaders excited with all the other benefits associated with another structure. The most common Hybrid binary is when the companies pair up the Binary with a Unilevel, creating unique synergy while creating long term profitability.

BINARY: THE PROS

The positives within a binary plan are directly associated to the characteristics of support that it creates. Within a binary, every distributor that is placed within an organization has the ability to create a larger team for other distributors, creating a sense of teamwork and support throughout the team. Unlike in the Unilevel, where the leader is sometimes encouraged to personally enroll and keep their placement close to themselves, in the binary, they are actually forced to pick somewhere in the tree and place them – in turn helping other people build their businesses at the same time. The binary creates a great opportunity for unity within an organization, and gets the people excited who sometimes wouldn't normally get excited. Even when the increase in organization isn't increasing the earnings of a person in the binary, it can still be exciting to watch a team grow – and can increase the perception of future potential.

For those of us who have taught compensation plans, we have found that binaries are also some of the easiest and simplest plans to teach, and therefore, there is sometimes stronger duplication in the field. Both of these positives can also attribute to the slightly higher retention that can be seen in binaries. People love the simplicity, and people have a hard time leaving when they see growth under them (regardless of whether it means anything financially or not).

BINARY: THE CONS

Every binary structure has limitation on the earnings that individuals can make within a single position. These limits actually are the very things that make the binary possible, and help create the human behavior that makes the binary financially stable. These limitations can, at times, be perceived to be cumbersome, and can also create a lot of animosity with the field and between the associates and the company. Yet, these limitations, although necessary, are rarely seen as a good thing by those who are being limited by them.

Within binaries, there is also a high degree of emotion that becomes involved relatively quickly. People learn the power and potential of unity with a binary and often times walk into the organization with high expectations of the team above them to develop things to happen under them. These magic organizations that are supposed to appear out of little or no effort on their part rarely appear, but are regularly expected. This sometimes can yield frustration within a team who has high expectations and gets little. Yet, to make this worse, there will be times when someone will be positioned better in the organization to have support from a more active upline, and this will just fuel the flames of others in the group who may feel it is less fair that they were not positioned in a similar spot. In binaries, it is often much harder to train people to stop looking around at other organizations to see what is happening, and to just start looking at your own organization and identify what can happen.

BINARY: LIFESPAN

The lifespan of the binary is really only as good as its product, management, and marketing. The binary plan can be stable enough (as long as it is not a cycle binary) to really allow the rest of the company to determine its own success. If structured and created properly, the binary plan can last a long time in domestic markets, and can allow the product to be introduced into a number of homes worldwide.

If the plan is a cycle binary, there is a high likelihood that the plan will need to change – not only adjust, but change to a different type of binary. All the other binary types should be considered stable as long as they are appropriately managed within the corporate environment, and there are minimal risky decisions made in relation to the plan in an attempt to be unique or more marketable.

The only real risk is mismanagement and improperly audited expansion or promotions. Often times, new companies with binaries will create promotions that will actually create a high risk of failure within the rest of the plan.

Also, as companies expand, they usually want to go into international markets, a number of which will be very good at decreasing the human breakage ratio. If not properly evaluated when moving into these international markets, binary plans have the potential to put all the company's markets at risk, depending upon the structure and placement of the other bonuses associated with the binary plan.

BINARY: BUILDING STRATEGIES

Just like any other compensation plan, the building strategies that coincide with the binary are different with each variation that exists. Here are some general thoughts for each variation.

Cycle Binaries

When building a Cycle Binary, you are pretty much concerned only with the volume between the two teams and not as much concerned about the placements. So there are two ways of thinking when building a cycle binary.

The first way is to build the cycle binary in a matrix fashion, where you just try to fill out the two-by-two-by-two organization within your team. What this does is give you the same check you would get otherwise, but it helps your top people also build a check, potentially increasing retention. As a result, you may get some laziness and lack of activity from these team members. This will also increase the amount of payout, significantly increasing the likelihood that the plan will be maxed quicker and require a change instigated by corporate – but your team may grow quicker.

The second way of thinking is to only build straight lines within your two teams. By building straight lines, you are able to help everyone a little and encourage them to engage and build the other side of their own organization in order to build a team. This way of building creates the same amount of earnings for you, less earnings for your team, but creates much more duplication and motivation for your team to grow.

Business Center Binaries

Once you identify that it is a Business Center Binary, by pretty much requiring someone to work more than one position within the organization to actually make a significant income, you need to identify how you are able to get those additional business centers. Some companies will give them to you when you achieve rank, and some companies will ask that you buy the additional business centers at the time of enrollment or after you max the earnings of a business center. If they ask you to buy the additional business centers at the time of enrollment – do it! If they do not ask you to buy them, but you get the feeling that you may need them in the future anyway – do it!

125

When you first enroll in these business center binaries, buying your own spot, and then purchasing two additional spots - one on each of your binary legs - can help you exceedingly in the future. Some companies will allow this purchase at the beginning, and some companies will not officially allow you to do this without purchasing or enrolling these spots under different names. Either way, acquiring these spots in these old-school Business Center Binaries can be extremely helpful in the future, whether you will need them or not.

After purchasing these additional spots, many people get confused about how to build three spots at the same time. The reality is the best way to utilize these spots is to ignore that these additional spots exist when you start building. Once you have acquired your three spots, you only worry about building your first spot; and you start to build two legs (preferably straight lines). Only after you are half way to maximizing your first spot do you start to build your other two spots. At this point, each of those spots will already be half way built, because each will already have a strong leg that you built out when building your first position. Then you begin to build two legs again, but you are now building one leg under each of these spots (opposite to the leg that is already built out). By keeping the momentum of building two legs, you are able to help maximize these spots quicker as well; and in the process of maximizing the second and third spot, you help to complete the maximization of the first.

The timing that you move into building the second and third spot is critical. If you wait too long to start building your second and third spot, and the first spot is already maximized, then your activity in those additional spots will still benefit you, but will not benefit that original position because you are already maximized. If you start building too early, you will find yourself neglecting the original two legs you were supposed to build, and you will find yourself building all four legs (the two legs under the two positions) at the same time, splitting the momentum and unity of the binary, ultimately making it more difficult.

Hybrid Binary

Building a Hybrid binary effectively has two simple phases. Most people believe that building compensation plans need to be confusing and involved; but this is not true with a hybrid binary. For most people, only the first phase will apply, but I warn you that the down fall of many people in Hybrid Binaries is attempting to move to the second phase too soon. Nevertheless, I will describe both phases, trusting that the reader will be able to temperance themselves from the second phase until reasonable.

Phase 1 – In starting to build your Hybrid Binary, it is preferred that you start building in straight lines down both of your legs. By building in straight lines down both of your legs, each enrollment that is placed on the bottom of that leg has the potential to aid and help build the business and the unity of the entire team that you have been working on. Because most hybrid binaries are commissioned from a percentage from the lesser of the two legs, building in a straight line may not only increase your check, but it will increase your entire team's potential. Phase 1 is as simple as that.

Now, there is a temptation with binary plans, when you enroll a good friend or someone that you *know* will do the business, you may feel the need to help support and encourage their business. This may lead you to want to place one of your enrollments on your inside leg, instead of at the bottom of the organization, in an attempt to *support* them. This is a temptation because everyone wants to seem nice, and they want to be supportive in this industry – and they know that in order to succeed, they need to be supportive. Yet, let's consider the potential long-term results of this action.

By placing an enrollment in under another distributor's inside leg (not part of the straight line), instead of at the bottom of the leg, that enrollment is only benefitting that one person instead of the whole team that it could have helped support. Also, as a result, you have just placed your new enrollment in a sticky situation. Now, instead of your new enrollment having a whole team of upline support in building their business, they only have you and this one friend that you placed them under to help them. This usually means that at the end of the day, the new associate gets less support, and industry statistics show that this action actually decreases retention. Now the risk of attrition is involved, with a potential of losing your new distributor in the long run.

If, in the best case scenario, the new associate is excited to work, but this friend that you were positive was going to build the business decides not to build or to do something else, or to quit, you now have this associate lost in your organization with no support and no one in the upline who is likely to help them build their organization. That "no one in the upline" will more than likely include yourself, as you will have learned at this point that the best placement is to place your people on the outside straight legs, and you will not feel it wise to continue to place in this random position in the tree. It is very wise to stick with building on the outside until you are making a relatively significant income. Nevertheless, the point is you can never really tell who will build and who will not, and it is not worth risking a single enrollment by placing them in an unsecured position without proper upline support.

Now that Phase 1 is defined, we can move to Phase 2, but before I describe Phase 2 – I need to warn you. Phase 2 will sound funny after reading the warnings in Phase 1, but it works!

The only caveat is for the reasons detailed above, DO NOT PREMATURELY JUMP TO PHASE 2! There are a lot of people in this industry that believe if Phase 1 is good, then Phase 2 is better, and they will start with Phase 2, only to destroy their organization.

Phase 2 – After you are making a significant income with Phase 1, and your team has now grown relatively independent, your team has also matured, and those straight legs are also growing because you have trained your team to do that same thing, you can start to consider Phase 2. In Phase 2, you identify up to three people in each leg that you personally sponsored in your team that have really proven they are committed. These are people who have been through the good times and the hard times and are still building their organizations. They are people who have been in your organization, and at this point, without your assistance, have built and supported a good team on their own.

Now that you have identified these individuals on each side of your team, you are able to call these your "go to organizations". When you enroll someone new to the organization, you now take a few steps to identify where to place them (instead of just at the bottom of the leg). First, you identify which leg they need to go in to or the leg you are trying to build (usually the leg with the least amount of volume). Second, you look at your three leaders in that leg, and you pick one (it is usually a good idea to just go down the list in order, giving one to each of them in the order that you would like). Then, when you identify that leader, you will place them where *you* choose to place them on the inside (weak leg, or pay leg) of that individual – in an effort to increase that leader's check for the week.

Doing this action does a number of things: (1) It increases the leader's check, making him happier, and gives him a greater sense of support, unity, and commitment to you; (2) it still increases your weaker leg volume, and allows your Binary Earnings to increase just as if you had placed them at the bottom of that leg; (3) because you have also increased the earnings of someone you personally sponsored, you also usually increase your earnings of whatever other bonus structure is in the plan that classifies it as a hybrid plan (usually the matching or the unilevel payout). This gives you the maximum amount of financial and structural benefit in the long run.

Yet, after seeing all of these benefits, many people feel very anxious to jump to Phase 2, and they may do so at their own detriment. Remember, do not jump to Phase 2 too early. The only reason Phase 2 even works is because your team has grown and developed, and you have removed or filtered out those individuals who are not going to be in it for the long haul. The leg that you are placing your new enrollment in is going to be with a proven leader, and that leg is going to grow with, or without, your support (independent of your action); which minimizes the fear that the new enrollment will be left without support. The only reason why Phase 2 works is because it is only for the advanced organizations. Anyone who jumps too soon will find themselves working themselves out of an organization.

MATRIX: DEFINITION

Matrix structured compensation plans have the most forced structure to them of all the organization types. In a Matrix plan, it defines how many people can and MUST be on each level of each person, therefore there is a defined amount of spots available on each level of the organization. An easy way to think about matrixes is to think of the unilvel plans but with walls on the organization. You can have many levels deep, but you can only have so many people on each level.

The result of this is that after you have filled your first level, you are required now to enroll your next members on the second level, which in turns builds your first level associates organization. The most traditional, or common, matrix is what they call a "3 by 3" Matrix (which is what we will use for our examples in this text, but all of the principles are applicable to all the other matrix types). This means that you can have three people on your first level, and they can all have three people on their first level (which equals a total of nine people on your second level), and so on. The goal of the Matrix is to fill it out.

MATRIX: VARIATIONS

The variations or evolution of the matrix is all based on how the matrix rules are enforced through the building process and the end result of each of them. The three most common variations in the industry are: The Standard Matrix, The Forced Matrix, and The Overlaid Matrix.

The Standard Matrix

Within the Standard Matrix, the limitations on the organization are enforced, but there are still no requirements of placement. This means that you still can only build three people wide under each person, but you are not required to build your first three positions before you can start building in your second, third and fourth level. These plans do not require you to fill one level entirety before you can start building in another.

The Standard Matrix plan is really not much different than a standard unilvel plan with a few barriers. As you can often see in many unilevel marketing materials, they will talk about the power of network marketing, and can show the potential numbers of finding three people who do the same, and so on - in order to build a sustainable organization. These numbers are all true, but the Standard Matrix highly recommends that you build that way, with the limitations of not being able to step out of that structure (you cannot have four on a level).

The Forced Matrix

In a Forced Matrix, the associate is forced to build the matrix in the order of the available or open spots in the tree. When enrolling a new associate in your organization, you may not even be asked where you would like them placed in your organization, but they will be automatically placed within your tree in the nearest location in an effort to help fill out the matrix. In a Forced Matrix, you are required to have your first level full before you can build on your second, and your second before you can build on your third. The Forced Matrix has the highest level of enforced structure of any of the plan structures in the industry.

The Over Laid Matrix

As the years went on, and people eventually kept looking for more and more innovation in compensation plans, the Overlaid Matrix became possible. The Overlaid Matrix is a forced matrix with one significant difference. The organizations that are next to you in your placement in the tree will overflow with your own, or in other words, the other teams next to you will cascade into your own team. This creates a unique support, both from your upline, who is forced to help build you, but also creates a larger team from those surrounding you who are also forced to share their team with you.

For example, in a 3-by-3 Over Laid Matrix, you are required to have three people on your front level. The two distributors next to you in your organization are also required to have the same. As they fill in their three, one of their members flows into your organization. Their furthest right would become your furthest left in your organization, and now, as that member is building their organization, they are helping to fill out your matrix. This can happen on both sides of your organization. Over laid matrixes can be complex to understand – but as difficult as they are to generally understand when first presented, the internal difficulties create complexities that are impossible to describe adequately in such a short text.

THE MATRIX: THE PROS

The largest positive that results in the matrix is the level of excitement and the imagination that can be fueled during the initial presentation. When potential new associates are introduced to network marketing, and are excited about the potential, the matrix concept will always sell them and push them over the edge with enthusiasm. The marketability of the Matrix structure is off the charts, everyone loves the idea. When the potential new associate connects that there will be people above them building that may be required (and in the case of the Over Laid Matrix, people above them and to the side of them) to help build their business in order for them to succeed – it is over, they are in. The one and only positive about a Matrix plan is that it is a recruiting machine when trained in conjunction with the potential of network marketing.

THE MATRIX: THE CONS

As much as the Matrix plans are recruiting machines, that it really all they are good for. In fact, they are traditionally the most unstable of all plans – and rarely are sustainable in the long haul.

Simple math teaches us that for each level that fills out, there is a larger amount of distributors needed to fill out the next level. In the case of a 3 by 3, you need the following number of distributors in each level of the organization:

Level 1 – 3
Level 2 – 9
Level 3 – 27
Level 4 – 81
Level 5 – 243
Level 6 – 729
Level 7 – 2,187
Level 8 – 6,561
Level 9 – 19,683
Level 10 – 59,049

Now, these are the same numbers that can really excite someone in an organization, and they will be told that with this many people in their organization, they are bound to make a fortune. But when you look at these numbers from a different perspective, the company now needs to grow almost 60,000 new distributors to fill out their 10th level - (almost a 300% increase). Keep in mind that this company now needs to increase on average 300% a year just to keep up with the demand of filling out an additional level. Eventually this growth will lag, and the organization will begin to eat itself from the bottom up as retention will fall the way of failed expectations. Simple statistics and the power of 3 – the same things that create excitement for Matrix plans – ultimately prove its long-term error as well.

If you are at the bottom of one of these organizations, and you realize that you may need 60,000 more people in the company before you may have any granted support in building your business, you may feel rather taken advantage of – particularly when you compare it to those who got in at the beginning; many who may not have had to work to generate the organization they are benefiting from and you are contributing to.

Yet, those people who got in at the beginning may not be enjoying things as much either, at least in the long run, as they see their levels start to shrink. The shear growth and population required to sustain these organizations for the long term does not exist – and therefore people start to leave. First the bottom level leaves out of disappointment, and then the next level erodes, and the next – all the way up the tree until the company needs to wipe away the slate and start fresh again.

In addition to population needs, there is also a problem of laziness and expectations that is created in Matrix plans. Although it sounds much easier to recruit and build a matrix when you start, this is not always the case. As people realize the potential in the beginning, their expectations are that someone else will build the business or even be forced to build their business for them. It is actually much harder to create the incentive to build within a Matrix plan. Even the largest leaders in the industry will have motivation issues, and if you don't have anyone recruiting, but waiting for someone else to do it for you – then no one recruits, and nothing gets done.

Yet, this excitement can be rekindled by creating new variations, which is what the Over Laid Matrix attempted to do. The results of the Over Laid Matrix increased the amount of people who were supporting the growth of your organization, and therefore, it was easier to build and grow your team. This also helped slightly to overcome and delay the issues that revolved around the statistic requirement for the Matrix to grow – it meant that you wouldn't hit the population wall as soon, and delayed the inevitable for a longer period of time. So this created quite a bit of excitement in the industry- but one thing that they did ignore was the huge mass of data and literature and industry analysis from experts explaining the larger problem which the Over Laid Matrix exasterbated. The Over Laid Matrix is the most financially unstable structure in the industry to date.

Eventually, because of its recruiting capability and its overlaid organizations (where one team member can get equal credit from three different separate teams), the payout in the matrix would eventually exceed the available funds. No matter what commission percentage you tacked on to the compensation plan, the more successful the company was, the quicker it would break and financially shatter the plan. These plans are extremely unstable and require constant adjustments within the plan – eventually they will need to cap the amount paid to the distributors individually to a minimum to ensure that there will be funds available for growth within the organization. As these actions take place in an effort to foolishly stabilize the plan, the resulting distributing of funds will create low-paid leaders who will be sharing their pay with low-working distributors.

THE MATRIX: THE LIFESPAN

The lifespan of the Matrixes are short, but as for timeline it is more related to the size of the organization. The Matrix plans are the most sensitive to growth, and the larger they become, the shorter their lifespan is. This is one of those counter intuitive moments in network marketing where the more successful the idea is, the less stable it is at the same time; the more the Matrix grows and fills out, the less life it will continue to have. This is because, as stated above, the Matrix is all a numbers game, and there are only so many people in the world to continue the momentum necessary to keep things interesting in a Matrix, and once the momentum starts to dwindle, the organizations starts to erode that much faster.

Because of the lifespan of a Matrix plan, these plans are better matched with marketing products or fake products that have a limited lifespan themselves.

When you look into the industry, there really has only been one company that has had any longevity that started with a Matrix plan. There really has not been anyone who has lasted the test of time with these plans, and there is a reason for that. In fact, that one company that could be the poster child for the Matrix success really is only still around because they were able to successfully change their plan away from the Matrix after they got their momentum and merged it into a Unilevel. They planned it at just the right moment so that the commission checks were not negatively affected by the change, and therefore, had little repercussions within their organization from this change.

THE MATRIX: BUILDING STRATEGY

The most important thing you can know about building a Matrix is knowing that its lifespan is limited. This is why the marketed or fraud products match so well with these plans; because the best way to build your business with a Matrix is to maximize your limited time with the plan. Knowing that it will only last for a short while doesn't mean that you can't make money; it means that you can only make money for a short while and that you have the potential to make a lot of money in a short while. Also, knowing that it will end shortly can hasten your activity in building your organization and minimize your frustration when it is no longer the check that you may have become accustom to.

Matrixes are all about momentum and excitement. The strategy in building your Matrix is teaching people the concept and the importance of staying on Autoship or regularly placed orders. In most matrixes plans, there is nothing more than that, because the company dictates the actual placement. All of your strategy is in the presentation focusing on timing, pretending it will last forever, and selling the false impression that it will be easy money.

OTHER STRUCTURES

It wouldn't be entirely fair to pretend that these three structures are the only structures that exist within network marketing. They are only the most prevalent, and there is a reason for that. These structures have been tested, broken, fixed, built, worked, and have lasted the test of time. There are always new ideas that come out of the woodwork, and they will always generate some excitement; but usually they go away as fast as they came.

There have been times in my consulting career when trusted friends would come and ask my advice concerning entering into a new structure. I wish to give you the same advice that I would give them. "Wait. Sit on the sidelines and wait."

There is no loss in not jumping into the very first new structure of its kind, there is only risk. I say this because if the new structure is a booming success, then it is only a matter of time after it is proven that someone else will generate a plan off of the same concept, but only more perfected and proven at that point. It is kind of like the electronics market: you never buy the first generation of anything, you allow the first generation to work out all of the bugs, and you buy the second generation.

By sitting back and waiting, you will not lose money, but you more than likely would lose money by jumping in, and even worse, you could lose your relationships and your network at the same time.

OTHER BONUSES

The fact is that as much as the structure of the plan generates the building culture of the company, it usually doesn't always generate the largest portion of the checks that are earned. Every compensation plan has a number of other bonuses worth considering or being aware of. These might be Fast Start Bonuses, recruiting or enrollment bonuses, leadership pools, generational payouts, matching, or bonuses that reward you for building in a particular way. This text has been designed to be a simple approach to evaluating companies, and there is nothing simple about the evaluation of these bonuses that could be detailed in such a text as this one. As much as there would be many that would argue with me, the things detailed in this text already are much more important to consider when looking at a network marketing opportunity than the other bonus types in question.

For those of you who are looking for some more in-depth and complex readings on these types of bonuses, I would refer you to another text written for the corporate environment. *Common Mistakes in Network Marketing Compensation Plans* is a text designed to help corporate management identify the most common and prevalent errors in the industry during the creating or management of a compensation plan in order to avoid them. That text could also be used when evaluating a compensation plan more intensely in identifying if the company has made any of those errors.

Thoughts to take away from this chapter:
- The three primary types of structures that define culture and building technique are: Unilevel, Binary and Matrix.

- Understanding Compression is the key to understanding Unilevel Plans.
- Each Binary Plan type has very different building techniques and stability rates.
- Matrix Plans are the most unstable plans in the industry.
- When unique, unproven structure ideas present themselves, WAIT, and see how they fair in the future.

CHAPTER 8

CORPORATE TEAM:
FOUNDERS, MANAGEMENT, AND
EXPERIENCE

You would not believe the wide variety of people that decide they are going to start or run a network marketing company. There are people who have millions who are willing to put it all on the line for it, and there are people who have nothing who are trying to run something out of their garage. There are people with experience and no money, and there are people with money and no experience, all with the dream that they can succeed in one of the most increasingly competitive markets in the world.

Now, there are stories in the industry of remarkable success from the garage, or management teams gaining experience through the experience of starting their own company. These stories excite investors and people alike, and they are true stories. Unfortunately, these stories are very few in comparison to those who try and have not come out of the last decade; the stories that are heard about massive success out of nothing in the corporate world is a collection of legends that all developed over the last thirty to forty years.

The industry has changed, and I dare say it is no longer possible for someone to fall into success as those legendary stories allude to. On a corporate level, it is more competitive than ever, and any lack of experience, funding, or personality can weaken the whole ship, and bring it down to the depths of the sea.

It is therefore also no wonder that the current climate today within the network marketing industry has produced equally legendary stories of failure in the last decade. Just as there are stories of success from nothing in the distant past, more recently, there are stories of companies with all of the capital in the world and no profit to show for it. Today there are products or services that can save lives (or to be more politically correct – increase the standard of health in the lives of millions), but can't find the leadership to be able to share it with the world. Even amazing products with awesome executive teams and good funding, but one bad founder with an arrogant attitude and pride can intentionally push his company and his associates to failure. On paper, many of these scenarios can seem perfect, but the smallest weakness can affect the corporate environment, and, in turn, affect your ability to be successful as a distributor. Remember that at the end of the day, each Distributor is placing the future of their business in the hands of those who run and manage the corporate environment. It is up to the corporate team that manages the operations of the product to ensure that they have your product in stock, that it is being delivered, that orders are received, and that commissions are paid. It is the company that gives the Distributor the opportunity to succeed, and without being aware of the team behind the company image, or the man behind the curtain, each distributor is placing their activity, actions, efforts, and future business at risk.

Those things that you are going to want to be aware of when you look at a corporate environment is going to be the Founders/Presidents, Investors, Management Team, the corporate culture or environment, and International Goals. The comments in regards to these topics can either send up significant red flags, or they can increase confidence in the choices that you have made.

FOUNDERS/PRESIDENT

The public Founders and the President of the company are going to be, and should be, the most seen persons in regard to the corporate environment. Their experience should be critical to the company and the potential the company has for success. The best way to predict the future when evaluating a business, or in this case, a President or Founder, is the past. Check the President's and Founder's past history of success; their "real" history of success. You would be surprised what "thirty years of experience" can mean when it is posted online.

There is also a need to try to identify how active the President or the Founders are in the day-to-day operations of the company. There are two types of these positions: show positions and leading positions. There are many presidents who are only given the position for show and to give a legitimate name to the company. These types of Presidents are not necessarily a bad things, because it can give you a greater presence in the market for his namesake, although it makes it all the more critical to understand the experience and abilities of the Management Team who is really running the company. Yet, at the same time, it should be noted that the less the Founder or President is involved in the company, the less aware they are of what is actually happening, which can cause strain in the company as they still usually have significant pull in important decisions. Often times, this can be a liability to have someone making decisions without a presence in the environment.

Leading positioned Presidents are those who are in the day-to-day affairs of the company, and are in the corporate office every day. These are the Presidents who have the pulse of the company and really are engaged. With these types of Presidents or Founders, to know them is to know the company. Their feelings, impressions, goals, and expectations for the company are going to be disseminated among the company. The company will be as safe as they are. In these circumstances, know them as best as you can to determine what they are capable of.

With all that said, like so many things in Network Marketing, a President or the Founders cannot necessarily make a company successful, but they have the most power to make it fail. It is within these positions that you will most likely find the type of dangerous pride and narcissism that has the potential to take a company down all for the sake of proving a point. If you sense any of that from any of the Founders or President, I would strongly reconsider working with that company. There is nothing more painful than giving your time, talents, and efforts in building your business, only to have someone else be willing to kill their business – and take yours down with them.

INVESTORS

Identifying who the investors or owners of the company are is often not openly discussed outside of the corporate environment, but for the same reasons, if it is discussed in the corporate environment, it should be discussed in the field as well. Who owns the company can sometimes mean much more than who is running the company. At the end of the day, whoever has the money or owns the company is the person who has the final word. This is the real boss!

In today's environment there are traditionally three sources of funding: privately funded, self funded, and funded through capitalist investor groups. Each of these funding types carries its own risk, but each funding type also has its own emphasis in stability; and it is worth it to briefly review each of these and the effects it can have on the corporate environment with the potential liability.

Privately funded companies can be seen as some of the most risky funding for the distributor. This means that there is usually one or two individuals, who are not identified, who are funding the company. These people are usually not the ones running the company, but are "silent" partners. The reality is that they might be silent in the marketing literature, but they are rarely silent in the corporate environment. Private investors carry with them their own expectations of success within the industry, and have often been sold on promises of remarkable returns that are rarely seen in the expected time frames (from the legendary success stories of the past). They can also be the most emotional and sensitive with their money. The more involved they may be in the company, the more damage they can be as "Cash is King", and they will always rule in the decisions, which often times can be counterproductive to the success of their own company.

Self funded capital is usually the best and safest. This means that the management team themselves have decided to fund it on their own. These are the people who are working in the corporate environment, and they now have a significant investment in the success of the company. This can yield some remarkable decisions, and some of the greatest companies. There is little risk of someone stepping in and making an executive decision without perspective, and there is little risk of a sudden withdrawal of funding. These are the companies that can have the most stability, as long as the investing management has the appropriate capital necessary to actually get a company rolling. The one downfall of these self funded companies is the lack of funds; they often extremely underestimate the amount of money or time it really takes to get things started, and when the funding runs out, they start looking for other investors.

Investment Capitalist Groups can be a good thing and a bad thing, depending on the group and the executive management team of the company. This is usually a group of investors that have pooled their money together to create a company that goes and invests in other companies. They have experienced employees to evaluate the investments and approve it. These can be good because there is usually not one or two investors, but a whole group, and the company is less likely to get edicts from above in decisions that affect the distributor force directly. This is because when they invest in the company, they are also investing in the management team, and trusting them to get the company rolling and in good shape. These investors will often just come in and buy a chunk of the company for additional capital and play it as equity - taking a chunk of the future retained earnings.

The risk within this investment type is the push to make their money back as quickly as possible; the investment capitalist group now has extremely strict expectations on their return and the timeline thereof. They are in the business of making money, and sometimes (often times) they can pressure the executive teams of these companies to make decisions to increase profits or the bottom line, which may not be good in the long run for either the distributor force or the corporate environment. There are many network marketing companies in recent years that have created a blue print of massive success that is not sustainable. These companies were fully aware of that blueprint, but were doing it as a result of the pressure to gain as great a return on an investment as quickly as possible; and they disregarded the longevity necessary for a stable distributor force. It is these examples that make knowing where the investment or ownership of a company lies.

TWO YEAR TIMELINE

Yet, despite the final funding source, it is important to note that if you are looking at a start up or new company, the company really only has two years to become profitable. At that point, any investor (private, self, or capitalist) will usually pull the funding. No one likes to lose money for two years.

Now, if the company can be self sufficient by two years, they usually can bide their time and hope that they continue to grow. This means that if a company has been around two years, you can almost assume that they are at least breaking even, and as long as they continue to grow, they will be there. The further and further passed that two year mark, the more stable it is traditionally considered.

The further and further away they are from hitting the two year mark, the more and more critical the distributor needs to be aware of every area evaluated in this book, and particularly this chapter to identify if they will make it past that two year review from their investors.

MANAGEMENT TEAM

At the end of the day, the management team is going to have a tremendous effect on the stability of the organization. No matter how great or well experienced the Founders or President are, they have flaws, weaknesses, and an inability to do everything themselves. Good Presidents will learn quickly that they will only be as good as the people they surround themselves by, and therefore, the experience that they surround themselves with in the Executive and Management teams can give a direct reflection on the President's ability to lead and their necessary level of humility.

When evaluating the management team of the company, the only rule is to use common sense. Ask about each major member's experience in the industry, education, successes, failures, and even relationship to other members within the management or executive team.

The key positions to evaluate are going to be each of the Executive Management team (including any Chief Officers and Vice Presidents) and any Directors. Is the Customer Relations Director there because they have superior skills and will help service your team better, or because they are the son-in-law of a Founder (or worse an Investor)? Do they actually have someone with experience running, managing, auditing, and analyzing the compensation plan, or are they just hoping it will just work? Does their Operations Officer have experience in managing all the moving parts of a manufacturing line, as well as staffing an office? Without any of these hinges, the door to success (both in the corporate team as well as in the field) will not only be hard to open, but will be jammed shut!

At the end of the day, a management team should be doing three things in a network marketing company: (1) placing orders and providing customer support, (2) shipping products, because they are in stock and are of quality, and (3) paying commissions accurately and on time. When looking at your management team, you should be evaluating the track record for each of these components or the likelihood that they will succeed with their current staff.

CORPORATE CULTURE AND ENVIRONMENT

This may sound like a small thing, and it is in the big picture, but I think that many people would be surprised when they feel the effects of the corporate culture in their sales organization. The corporate culture consists of how the company (Founders, President, and Management) is treated, and in turn, treats their employees. The environment that the managers produce in the company will directly be felt by your team when they call into Customer Service, when people go to meetings and events, or even when they attend a convention. When the employees enjoy working for a company, your team can feel that, and they can be more secure in their own emotions towards the company they have chosen. A positive corporate environment is a positive thing to have.

INTERNATIONAL GOALS

There is nothing to say here but total bluntness (and I suspect that these comments are more directed towards the few corporate executives who may be reading this). International expansion too soon, FAILS! International Expansion too quickly FAILS! Too much international expansion FAILS! The average rate of international expansion in the industry FAILS!

The speed at which a company is planning to grow internationally can directly reflect the experience that a company has and the potential the company has to succeed. Many people expect a consultant to say that international expansion is the key to long-term global success – and they would be wrong. International expansion takes time, money, and lots of experience that even some of the largest companies do not have. Many international markets that are profitable for large companies are only profitable because of the infrastructure that the market is taking from the home market. Without massive success in the home country, most international markets would never break even. In fact, the largest and most successful companies who have been "successful" in international expansion only have a quarter of their international markets ever reach profitability.

With this fact in mind, I always find it humorous when a two year old company is boasting that they are in thirty markets. This means that internally, all of their resources are being used just to stay afloat as a whole instead of trying to grow a single market to mass profits. Most of these companies will fail due to international expansion, or even worse, will be a sign of a failing company. Many companies attempt to go international out of desperation with the hopes and prayers that something will happen in another country that is not happening in their home market.

Sometimes the company will try to move into the market within three months. This is never a good idea. Companies sometimes forget that the other country is a whole different market, with a different culture, different currency, different laws and regulations, and different likes and dislikes socially. Opening a new country for a network marketing company successfully is really like opening a brand new company in a whole new world, and should be treated as such.

Be concerned if the company is moving too fast into international waters or starting and finishing the project too quickly. Many US based markets crumble because an investment was made in a foreign market which failed and drained the resources and finances of the home market, forcing the company to close its doors or be sold.

Thoughts to take away from this chapter:
- Take the time to be aware of the team behind the curtain.

- Know as much as you can about the Founders and President of the company.
- Know as much as you can about the ownership and investors for the company.
- Understand that each company has a two year window to succeed – and take that into consideration with any evaluation.
- Learn about the rest of the management team.
- Be wary of desperate or ill-considered international expansion.

CHAPTER 9

CONCLUSION: SELECTION, RECOMMENDATIONS, AND ACTIONS

Now, throughout this entire text, there has been enough information presented to hopefully allow any potential Distributor to properly evaluate any opportunity or network marketing company. It is also understood that each individual is different, and each person will place more or less importance on the different subjects that are presented. It is, therefore, an "easy out" to say that there is no perfect company for everyone, only a best company for each individual. Out of this text, take what is important to you, and weigh that portion of the evaluation more heavily. If you care more about product and stability, consider those aspects throughout your entire evaluation; if you care more about massive growth and quick income, then there are also considerations in making that decision within this text.

The key and ultimate purpose of this text is to increase your confidence in either the decision that you will make or the decision you have already made in your network marketing company of choice; or even better, if you recall the first chapter, it is to help you maybe understand why a previous endeavor into network marketing wasn't the right endeavor for you. And with that understanding, the fact that there still might be a great opportunity out there for you that will help you increase your residual income and help you find success.

LISTEN TO SUCCESS

Now, when you have decided or selected your company, there are some recommendations that might help you find success. It is interesting that whenever there is a new endeavor in anyone's life, there is always advice from the inexperienced. The single most important advice that anyone (me included) can give you is to respect, listen to, and learn from those who have worked and earned their success in the industry.

Find those who have succeeded in network marketing, and learn from them the *how-to's*. Whenever anyone wants to learn plumbing, do they go to their neighbor or a plumber? When someone wants to learn to be a doctor, do they learn from someone they met on the street or from a doctor? These answers should be simple. The point is, when you want to learn about being a successful network marketer within your selected company, you need to learn from those who are successful in that company – not from someone who is not successful.

Learn what they do, what they say, and how they build their business. Don't learn from the call center, your direct-sponsor neighbor, or even the corporate sales team (unless they also have great experience in being a network marketing distributor – which is rare). If they haven't succeeded in the field, then they don't understand what it takes to succeed, or how to do it.

I was once told that if you want to be the best, you have to learn from the best, and that has been the best advice that I have ever been given; and probably the best advice that I could ever give.

With that said, the rest of this chapter is going to contain some recommendations that I can make in helping you build your business. What you will notice is that they will not tell you how to build your business, teach a compensation plan, make a sale, or even find prospects. The reason you will not see this information in this chapter is because, even though I have consulted with some of the industry's largest leaders, the most experienced corporate staff, and even helped run successful network marketing companies, I have never built an at-home-based Distributor business on my own. Therefore, I will not pretend that I am the exception to the rule explained above.

What you will see in the rest of this chapter are recommendations of things that the most successful people in the industry have taught me, their teams, and have lived in their own lives that have helped them to be successful people, and therefore, aid in their network marketing. These are things that can help create a proper perspective that often is the most necessary thing in network marketing. These are things that I have learned and applied in my own life that have made me more successful in every facet; and therefore, I have also seen these same lessons aid numerous people in their lives, including their network marketing business. Learn and apply what you can from the rest of this chapter; and then go and learn what you can from the best in the industry.

STAY

When you have selected a company that you feel good about, the best thing you can do is commit yourself to that company and stay there. Remember, it was discussed within the first few chapters that most people (normal people) only really have one solid attempt at success in the industry before they burn out and quit the industry as a whole. The best chance you have at succeeding within network marketing is making one attempt and sticking with it.

When sticking with it, this can often mean that it can take months or years longer than expected to build a residual income. This is okay, and this is healthy. Keep it in mind that if, at the end of the year, you are only making an additional few hundred dollars a month in residual income, then that is a few hundred dollars extra that you otherwise wouldn't have had. The fact also is that if you stick with it and continue on that trend, that few hundred dollars can grow into a few thousand by the end of the second year. Sure, it is not fast riches, but that kind of money can completely change a family's standard of living for the long run.

Too many people quit too soon. Too many people get disappointed too soon. Too many people get in to one company only to start looking for the next company that might have the "better opportunity". If a person begins to build in one company only to reset themselves by starting in another company a few months or years later, then they only cut their chance of success in half with every move.

Now, with all of that said, this is not to say that if you have already tried and quit the industry, you have missed your chance. All that means is that you may not have been given your fair chance to succeed, or the right opportunity. What this text does is place the responsibility of finding that opportunity that works for you in your hands.

THE DALE CARNEGIE RULE

Dale Carnegie is one of the greatest writers and minds in applicable human relations within the recent century. His writings, as aged as they are, are still the standards and the blue print for nearly every book on the subject. If it were up to me, every person, both inside and outside of network marketing, would read each of his texts. This one act would change the relationships that each of us have and the way we live each of our lives. I cannot speak enough about how his texts have changed my own life and the lives of those who have read and applied his writings.

He is most known for his text *How to Win Friends and Influence People*. Within this text, he teaches each individual standard rules about developing relationships with others. Rules like:

- Never criticize, condemn, or complain
- Give sincere appreciation
- Smile
- Use an individual's name
- Be a good listener
- And many, many more!

Yet, with all these rules, there is one common theme within each chapter; and this theme is what I call *The Dale Carnegie Rule*. Throughout his entire text, with every tip, trick or trade, he attempts to teach, that he emphasizes the need to be SINCERE in each action we take. It is not enough to give a compliment, it needs to be sincere. It is not enough to smile at someone, it needs to be genuine. It is not enough to listen, it needs to be receptive listening. And the use of an individual's name is patronizing if it isn't said with affection.

The Dale Carnegie Rule is to be sincere in your actions. Be real when building your business. Be who you are, and when you talk to people, talk to people, not prospects. Live the Dale Carnegie Rule in everything that you do, and everything you do will be better for it.

STUDY THE INDUSTRY

To be successful at anything, you need to learn as much as you can about it. Again, if you want to be a doctor, do you just sign up for med school and consider yourself a doctor? Equally, many people in network marketing believe that they can just sign up in a company and expect to be a network marketer. It takes time and training.

This can mean that you need to learn from your leaders, and learn from those who have succeeded. This also can mean that you may need to read about the subject, and continue to do so as you grow through your experiences and the application of what you learn.

INVEST IN YOUR BUSINESS

The most successful network marketers in the industry have learned to treat their business like a real business. They invest time and money into it in order for them to expect a reasonable return. Most normal businesses do not, or cannot, expect a profitable return within the first two years. Within network marketing, a profitable return can be reached within the first month or week, but this can be misleading. If that money was reinvested back into the business instead of being considered profit, the next check can be that much larger – and because it is a residual increase, all of your future earnings can increase with each reinvestment. Learning to take your earnings and reinvest into your business usually only brings larger profits for the future.

This can mean purchasing more inventory if that is how you generate your business. It can also mean buying more leads, attending more trainings, funding your own promotions, or helping your team grow. Identify what activities help your organization grow, and fund those actions or behavior. This investment is a real investment, and often comes with a real return.

MORE THAN THE 95%

There are some interesting statistics within the network marketing industry about who makes money and who does not make money. The most interesting thing is that the end result is the same lesson we learn throughout all of life: if you want more than most people, you only need to do more than most people.

If you want to make what the top 5% make in the network marketing industry, then you only need to work harder than 95% of the people. Now that might sound like a daunting task to some, but there is a secret to remember here: 95% of the people do not do much (if anything at all). If you want to make more than the 95%, then you only need to do more than the rest, and that isn't much. Putting forth a good degree of effort will usually put you within that top 5 percentile.

BECOME THAT PERSON

Within network marketing there is always a hope that as you go about your day-to-day experiences, you will come across the right person who will join your organization. Within these hopes, this special person will take the opportunity seriously and go to work. In the hopes and dreams of all network marketers, they look for the right person; the person that is going to take their team to the next level, drive volume, and build the business – in turn, building their business by being the sponsor of this hard working person. This is a real dream, where everyone wishes they can just get lucky and have someone, or a group of people, blow out the organization and build the business for them.

There are a few secrets here that may be worth considering. If you want that person in your team, you should realize you already have them: YOU! The best chance you will ever have to have that dream team member in your group is if you become that person in your group. Be active, be sincere, be busy building the business, and be that person that you are looking for.

What my mother always used to tell me when we would speak about marriage or hunting for a meaningful relationship was this: "Stop trying to find the right person, and start trying to be the right person." This is a universal truth in all principles when we look for "the right person" in any facet of our lives. If you can become the right person, you will grow and fill that role, and you will succeed; but most importantly, you will be in control of your own success, and you will be happy with what you achieve. You will have that person in your team, and your team will be what you want it to be.

There is another secret in this as well. When you become the right person, you will also attract similar people who are also "the right people." The more dedicated you are, the more dedicated the people you attract will be. The most dedicated, hard-working people in the world are not looking to partner up with someone who is not interested in working and having them do all the work; hard working people are looking for equally hard-working people to work hard with.

Now, of course, the next question is how to become the right person?

It takes three steps: identify, apply, and rely. First, identify all of the qualities in the person you would like to find to build your business for you, or to help you build your business. This might include hard-working, easy-learners and listeners, a student of the industry, and a willingness to get out of their com-

160

fort zone. Second, you apply those qualities in your own life. This can often take a lot of hard work, as well as developing temperance. Third, you then become reliable and consistent in maintaining your skills and continually developing them.

BE YOURSELF

At the end of the day, it is important to grow, develop, and become a better person, regardless of what you choose to do with your life. Yet, while achieving these goals, it is important to be yourself as you grow.

Be yourself as you grow in network marketing and as you select the company of your choice. Remember that the reason you are reading this book is to help you discover the company that will give YOU the greatest degree of success in relation to WHO YOU ARE. You don't necessarily need to change your whole personality to build a successful business, you only need to find the company that fits with you; and they are out there!

Thoughts to take away from this chapter:
- Listen to and learn from those who have succeeded in the industry.
- When you pick a company, STAY!
- Live The Dale Carnegie Rule: Be Sincere.
- Study the industry.
- Invest back into your business
- Do more than the 95% that are not doing anything.
- Stop looking for the right person and start becoming the right person.
- Be yourself.

About the Author

Ryan Daley is considered to be one of the most sought after corporate consultants within the network marketing industry. Using a combination of his experience through consulting with networkers and corporate executives, in running, writing, and managing compensation plans, and in conjunction with his education and study of behavior, he has developed a unique perspective and ability to see the industry in a holistic setting.

When receiving his Associates Degree in Behavioral Science, Ryan was honored as the Valedictorian. He also graduated Summa Cum Laude with a Bachelor Degree in Psychology from Utah Valley University. Ryan also studied for his Masters of Business Administration at the University of Utah while continuing his research on the *psychology of sales in an incentive-based environment (network marketing).*

Ryan has consulted directly with some of the largest leaders and earners within the network marketing industry, teaching them how to maximize their earnings within their respective compensation plan. He has developed many compensation plans, adjusted even more of them to gain stability, and managed the development of many commission engine implementations through a number of software packages. Using his experience, he has also directly consulted with numerous network marketing companies to aid in turning around or adjusting distributor behavior and increasing sales and company stability. He currently is a Vice President of one of the fastest-growing network marketing companies in history.

Ryan is married with two children, and loves his family.

Author can be reached at daleyconsulting@gmail.com

Made in the USA
Charleston, SC
20 April 2010